Essential
Ireland

by Penny Phenix

PASSPORT BOOKS
NTC/Contemporary Publishing Group

Page 1: *Arthurstown, Ballyhack harbour and castle, Co Wexford*

Page 5a: *Dan Foley's Pub, Anascaul, Co Kerry*
5b: *Girl with piglet at Dingle Farm, Peninsula World*

Page15a: *Jaunting car at Muckross Estate*
15b: *Cross at the sacred site of Clonmacnoise*

Page 27a: *Garinish Point, Beara Peninsula*
27b: *Kinsale local*

Page 91a: *Folk music at Bailey's Corner, Tralee*
91b: *Kilkenny pub sign*

Page 117a: *Celtic crosses, Inishmore, Aran Islands*
117b: *Iron way-marker near National Stud, Kildare*

Published by Passport Books, a division of NTC/Contemporary Publishing Group, Inc. 4255 West Touhy Avenue, Lincolnwood (Chicago), Illinois 60646–1975 U.S.A.

Copyright © The Automobile Association 1998
Maps © The Automobile Association 1998
Reprinted Oct 1998

Published by Passport Books in conjunction with The Automobile Association of Great Britain.

Written by Penny Phenix

Library of Congress Catalog Card Number: 97-76433
ISBN 0–8442–0138–3

Colour separation: BTB Digital Imaging, Whitchurch, Hampshire

Printed and bound in Italy by Printer Trento srl

The weather chart on **page 118** of this book is calibrated in °C. For conversion to °F simply use the following formula:

$$°F = 1.8 \times °C + 32$$

Contents

About this Book

KEY TO SYMBOLS

- ✚ map reference to the maps found in the What to See section
- ✉ address or location
- ☎ telephone number
- ④ opening times
- ⏹ restaurant or café on premises or near by
- ◎ nearest underground train station
- ▤ nearest bus/tram route
- ▤ nearest overground train station
- ⛴ ferry crossings and boat excursions
- ✈ travel by air
- ℹ tourist information
- ♿ facilities for visitors with disabilities
- ✋ admission charge
- ↔ other places of interest near by
- ❓ other practical information
- ➤ indicates the page where you will find a fuller description

Essential *Ireland* is divided into five sections to cover the most important aspects of your visit to the islands.

Viewing Ireland pages 5–14
An introduction to Ireland by the author.
Ireland's Features
Essence of Ireland
The Shaping of Ireland
Peace and Quiet
Ireland's Famous

Top Ten pages 15–26
The author's choice of the Top Ten places to see on the islands, listed in alphabetical order, each with practical information.

What to See pages 27–90
The four main areas of Ireland, each with its own brief introduction and an alphabetical listing of the main attractions.
Practical information
Snippets of 'Did you know...' information
4 suggested walks
4 suggested tours
3 features

Where To... pages 91–116
Detailed listings of the best places to eat, stay, shop, take the children and be entertained.

Practical Matters pages 117–24
A highly visual section containing essential travel information.

Maps
All map references are to the individual maps found in the What to See section of this guide.
For example, Dublin Castle has the reference ✚ 36B3 – indicating the page on which the map is located and the grid square in which the castle is to be found. A list of the maps that have been used in this travel guide can be found in the index.

Prices
Where appropriate, an indication of the cost of an establishment is given by £ signs:

£££ denotes higher prices, **££** denotes average prices, while **£** denotes lower charges.

Star Ratings
Most of the places described in this book have been given a separate rating:

✪✪✪	Do not miss
✪✪	Highly recommended
✪	Worth seeing

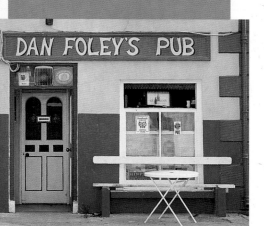

Viewing
Ireland

Above: *Dan Foley's Pub, Anascaul,
Co Kerry*
Right: *Girl with piglet at Dingle Farm,
Peninsula World*

Penny Phenix's Ireland

A Gentler Pace

Ireland is famous for its relaxed pace of life, and even in the cities, where there is much activity, there is an overall feeling that anything that can't be achieved today can easily wait until tomorrow. An Irishman was once asked if there was an equivalent Irish word to *Mañana*. 'Oh no', he replied, 'we have nothing with that sense of urgency!'

Traditional and Informal

Traditional music sessions are widespread throughout Ireland. Some city pubs will have them every night, with different musicians at each, and even in the country there will be a session somewhere within easy reach. Sessions are informal and unrehearsed, but the fiddlers, flautists, whistlers, pipers, *bodhrán* players and whoever else may turn up. All know the tunes and standards are very high.

Sheltered Strangford Lough in County Down is perfect for weekend sailing

It is not easy to define Ireland's attractions without resorting to clichés, but the simple fact is that only the very hard to please could fail to be captivated by Ireland and its people.

Celtic culture and heritage are very strong, and not just in the fine museums, arts centres and costumed banquets staged for tourists. There is renewed interest in the Gaelic language, with Gaelic radio and television stations and summer language schools in the Gaeltachts (Gaelic-speaking areas), and traditional music, once in danger of disappearing, is continuing its great revival. Like the music, Ireland can be calm and soothing or lively and exhilarating, depending on where you happen to be – in a remote valley amongst the mountains or enjoying 'the craic' in a traditional music pub.

In spite of this, do not expect to find people living in the past. The Republic of Ireland (sometimes called Eire) has enthusiastically embraced its membership of the EU and will grasp any opportunity for progress. Do not be surprised, for instance, if you discover that your friendly bed-and-breakfast hostess has a degree in marketing and tourism. Northern Ireland maintains a cheerful confidence in its many tourist attractions.

The 'Emerald Isle' is aptly named – the green pastures are almost incandescent in the sunshine that follows the rain, and though that rainfall is almost inevitable, it is a small price to pay for the beauties it brings – great rivers and lakes, tumbling streams and boglands rich in plantlife. Wherever you go, there is scenery that really does (if just one cliché can be allowed) take your breath away.

Ireland's Features

Geographical Information

- Ireland lies on the continental shelf to the west of the European mainland. To the east, over the Irish Sea, lies Britain, with Scotland 21km to the northeast.
- In area Ireland is: 7 million hectares and of those hectares 2.25 million are devoted to agriculture.
- The largest county is Cork and the smallest is Louth.
- The highest mountain is Carrantuohill 1,041m, in the Macgillicuddy's Reeks range of Co Kerry.
- The longest river is the Shannon at 340km, while the largest lake is Lough Neagh at 396sq km.
- Rainfall on the west coast averages 1300mm (but can exceed 2000mm in mountain areas); on the east coast, in the dryest area near Dublin, the maximum is 750mm.

Sport and Leisure

- Salmon Season: January to September.
- Brown Trout Season: 15 February to 12 October.
- Sea-Trout Fishing: June to September (or 12 October in some places).
- There is no close season for coarse fishing, and sea angling is possible all year round, depending upon weather conditions.
- Ireland has over 11,000 pubs.
- There are over 200 golf courses in Ireland.

Economic Factors

- **Alcohol** Bushmills, Jameson, Powers and Paddy whiskeys; Guinness, Beamish and Murphy's stout, Smithwick's beer; Cork gin; Baileys liqueur
- **Irish Linen** Banbridge Co Down is the main centre. The Ferguson Linen Centre has factory tours, and Banbridge is the starting point of Linen Tours, a coach journey around

nearby sites, including linen mills and factories. There is also an Irish Linen Centre in Lisburn.

- **Donegal Tweed** Magee & Co in Donegal town have been manufacturing tweed since 1866; Ardara Heritage Centre tells the story of Donegal tweed and Aran knitwear, and there are tours of hand-loom weaving centres.
- **Aran Sweaters** The distinctive patterns of the traditional Aran sweater are known all over the world. They are still produced in the Aran Islands.
- **Waterford Crystal** Waterford crystal is widely available throughout Ireland (and the world). The factory has organised tours (► 58).
- **Racehorses** Irish-bred racehorses are prized all over the world. Kildare is at the heart of horse-racing country and home of the National Stud. The great plain of The Curragh, stretching away to the west of the town, is dotted with stud farms, many in international ownership.

Ireland's most popular product dominates this Dublin scene

Animal Life

- There are over 55,000 horses in Ireland, of which some 15,000 are racehorses.
- Ireland has 27 mammal species, but only one reptile, the common lizard.
- There are no moles in Ireland.
- There are around 125 species of resident wild birds, and 250 species of visiting birds in Ireland.

Essence of Ireland

If your time in Ireland is limited, you will need to be selective, and one of the best ways of making your selections is by asking the locals. The conversations that will inevitably ensue will be as rewarding as the information you will glean. The essence of Ireland and the friendly good humour of the Irish people are inextricably linked.

Blakes Bar in Enniskillen is typical of Ireland's atmospheric town pubs

Ireland has great cities in each of its four quarters – Dublin in the east, Belfast in the north, Limerick and Galway in the west and Cork in the south – and just a short visit to each will demonstrate the differences in character between these regions.

THE **10** ESSENTIALS

If you only have a short time to visit Ireland, or would like to get a really complete picture of the country, here are the essentials:

• **Drive the Ring of Kerry** (▶ 54) to see some of Ireland's most spectacular coastal and inland scenery, including huge fjord-like bays, the country's highest mountain, sparkling lakes, pretty villages and colourful hedgerows and gardens which flourish in an exceptionally mild climate.

• **Join in a *ceilí*,** with traditional music and dancing to sweep you on to your feet.

• **Wander along Grafton Street in Dublin**, for the shops and the buskers, and have a coffee at Bewley's Café, a great Dublin institution, on the way.

• **Go to a race meeting at The Curragh.** The Irish have

the millions of emigrants who left this beautiful country for an unknown destiny in the New World.

• **Visit Skibbereen on the day of the cattle market** to sample the real working life of an agricultural community, but do not be in a hurry on the road because you will be following all manner of vehicles bringing livestock into town – all part of the experience.

• **For a taste of Ireland, eat oysters and drink Guinness** at Paddy Burke's Oyster Inn in Clarenbridge, famous for its oyster festival, or at Hooker Jimmy's on

a unique affinity with horses and a day at the races here is quite an experience.

• **Visit Glendalough** to soak up the atmosphere of this historic ruined monastic city in a beautiful valley of the Wicklow Mountains.

• **Look out from the Cliffs of Moher**, with no other landfall between here and North America, and contemplate the feelings of

the Quay in Galway where seafood is also a speciality.

• **Hire a cruiser and explore the lovely River Shannon**, its lakes and the historic sites, riverside towns and villages along the way.

• **Take a walk along the clifftops of Co Antrim to the Giant's Causeway** to see how ancient travellers would have first witnessed this most remarkable place.

Art and humour combine on this wall in Lisdoonvarna, Co Clare

9

The Shaping of Ireland

8000 BC
First settlement by hunters and fishermen.

4000 BC
The farming Gaels arrive and the Celtic language develops.

AD 350
Christianity reaches Ireland.

AD 432
St Patrick arrives in Ireland to begin his mission to convert the population to Christianity. The next three centuries see the foundation of many of Ireland's greatest monasteries and the production of wonderful illuminated manuscripts including the famous *Book of Kells* and the *Book of Durrow* both now in Trinity College Library in Dublin.

795
The Vikings invade Ireland, establish settlements at Dublin, Waterford and other coastal towns and introduce trade and the first coinage.

1014
High King of Ireland, Brian Ború, vanquishes the Vikings, but dies before he can achieve his aim of uniting Ireland.

1169
Ousted king Dermot MacMurrough invites the Anglo-Normans to help him regain his throne. They grasp the opportunity, and seize Ireland for themselves.

1541
Henry VIII forces Irish chiefs to surrender their land.

1558–1603
Elizabeth I tightens English hold on Ireland and establishes English and Scottish immigrants on land expropriated from the native Irish.

1595–1603
Rebellion led by Hugh O'Neill, Earl of Tyrone, fails after the Battle of Kinsale, resulting in the 'Flight of the Earls' (Irish aristocracy) to Europe.

1649
Cromwell conducts an aggressive campaign to impose his religion on the Irish, during which thousands of Irish are massacred. Cromwell's opponents have their land seized.

The capture of Wolfe Tone, the 18th-century revolutionary leader

1689
James II of England flees to Ireland after being deposed. He is finally defeated at the Battle of the Boyne by William of Orange, who became William III of England.

1691
The Treaty of Limerick heralds the ascendancy of the Protestant minority, who imposed severe restrictions on the Catholic majority.

1704
Penal Code introduced, which restricts Catholic land-owning and bans Catholics from voting, attending schools and military service.

1782
Ireland allowed its own parliament and a period of greater religious tolerance ensues.

1798
Wolfe Tone leads United Irishmen in an uprising, which is crushed.

1800
Ireland becomes part of Britain under the Act of Union.

1829
The Catholic Emancipation Act is passed.

1845–8
The Famine, brought about by the failure of potato crops, and widespread emigration because of the hardships, reduces the population by 2 million.

The cover of a momentous special issue of Irish Life

1916
The Easter Uprising leads to the execution of 16 leaders of the Irish Republican Brotherhood.

1920–1
Creation of the Irish Free State and separation of Northern Ireland (Ulster), resulting in Civil War between supporters and opponents of the Anglo-Irish Treaty.

1949
Creation of the Republic of Ireland (Eire).

1969
The start of the 'Troubles' in Northern Ireland, which remains part of the UK, following rioting between Catholics and Protestants during the annual Apprentice Boys' March in Londonderry. British troops are called in to keep the peace. The Provisional IRA launches a campaign of violence.

1972
The Republic joins the European Community.

1985
Anglo-Irish Agreement, signed by British Prime Minister Margaret Thatcher and Garrett Fitzgerald, the Irish *Taoiseach* (Prime Minister), gives the Republic of Ireland some involvement in Northern Ireland affairs.

Peace & Quiet

Getting away from it all in Ireland is not a difficult thing to do. Even from the centres of its largest towns and cities there are tantalising glimpses of remote hilltops, and within a half-hour drive of Dublin or Belfast, you could be standing in complete isolation, surrounded by some of the most beautiful scenery in the country.

Around the Coast

Ireland has some of Europe's emptiest and cleanest beaches, with great expanses of silvery sands and little rocky coves. The Donegal coast is renowned for its wonderful beaches, such as those at Bundoran, Creeslough, Fintragh Bay, Portnoo and Rathmullan. In Sligo those at Enniscrone, Mullaghmore and Rosses Point are among the best, while the south has the huge Barley Cove, and fine beaches around Youghal. Swathes of sand stretch all along the east coast, and in the north Benone Strand extends for 11km, backed by cliffs and dunes. Cranfield Beach, south of Kilkeel, is said to have the warmest water in the north.

The beach at Cougher on the Dingle Peninsula

Birdwatchers head for the great river estuaries, such as Strangford Lough, near Belfast, and the Shannon estuary in the west, where the mudflats are teeming with feeding birds. Offshore islands offer the most exciting sightings, particularly Rathlin Island in the north, the Saltee Islands off the south-eastern corner and Cape Clear in the south-west. And do not miss the Cliffs of Moher (▶ 67).

Inland Waterways

There are thousands of lakes in Ireland, particularly in the 'lakeland counties' which extend southwards from the border with Northern Ireland and in Connemara. Lough Neagh in Northern Ireland is the largest lake of all, and contains two fish which are almost exclusive to these waters – the pollan and the dollaghan. The wide Rivers Erne and Shannon, which widen even further into beautiful lakes as they flow seaward, are popular for cruiser holidays, and all of Ireland's lovely rivers are tranquil.

National Parks and Forest Parks

The large number of nature reserves all over Ireland are rich in animal and plant life, and the National Parks preserve some large areas of great beauty. Killarney National Park includes the most extensive areas of natural woodland remaining in Ireland. The Glenveagh National Park in Co Donegal consists of beautiful mountains, lakes, glens and woods, with a herd of red deer, and the Connemara National Park in Co Galway is very special.

There are great Forest Parks too, many with visitor centres, waymarked walks, scenic drives and picnic places. In Northern Ireland, Tollymore in the Mountains of Mourne, Castlewellan Forest Park and Gortin Glen in the Sperrin Mountains are particularly popular; in the Republic, Glengarriff Forest Park in the Beara Peninsula is among the finest, and the one near Rathdrum has one of Europe's finest collections of trees.

Gardens

Ireland's mild climate is a great boon to its gardeners, particularly in the west, where the Gulf Stream lengthens the flowering season and makes all kinds of things possible. The Sub-Tropical Gardens on Garinish Island off the Beara Peninsula (► 52) are a spectacular example. The stately homes of Ireland are enhanced by their gardens too. Those at Powerscourt, just south of Dublin, are among the finest in Europe, and in Northern Ireland Mount Stewart Gardens and Rowallane are exceptional among the National Trust's many properties there.

The attractive little town of Clifden is surrounded by spectacular Connemara scenery

Ireland's Famous

Words and Images
Irish subjects are increasingly attracting the film industry's moguls, including *The Crying Game*, *In the Name of the Father* and *Michael Collins*. *The Field*, filmed at Leenane in Connemara in the early 1990s, starring Richard Harris and John Hurt, was a surprise success. Less famous, but offering a compelling insight into life in the west of Ireland, was *Man of Aran*, made by Irish-American director Robert Flaherty in 1934.

Blarney
Words have always been important to the Irish. Around the time of the birth of Christ, the Celts were described by the Greek geographer Strabo as being fond of 'wordy disputes' and 'bombastic self-dramatisation'. Later, in Elizabethan times, the Earl of Blarney so infuriated the queen with his lengthy but empty promises that she declared 'I will have no more of this Blarney talk', coining the phrase long before kissing the Blarney Stone came into vogue.

For a small country, Ireland has more than its fair share of exceptional talent. Few other countries of this size can boast of so many internationally recognised names.

Stage and Screen
Irish actors have for many years found much favour with the great studios of Hollywood and major stars include Liam Neeson, Daniel Day Lewis, Kenneth Branagh, Stephen Rea, Peter O'Toole and Richard Harris, not to mention countless Americans with Irish connections, such as Martin Sheen, whose mother came from Borrisokane in Co Tipperary.

Music
Many Irish musicians and singers have found their way on to the international stage. Irish tenors were enormously popular in the early part of this century, and the names of Joseph Locke and John McCormick were known far beyond their native shores. More recently the world of rock music has included a strong contingent of Irish bands and soloists, such as Bob Geldof's Boomtown Rats, Van Morrison, U2, The Cranberries, Boyzone, The Waterboys, Paul Brady, Enya, Chris de Burgh and Sinead O'Connor. Traditional music has been taken all over the world by The Chieftains, and Riverdance, which showcases Irish traditional dance, has been a remarkable international success. In the realm of classical music, the flautist James Galway has international stature.

The World of Literature
Even before the written word, Ireland had a strong tradition of storytelling, and Irish writers are among the most acclaimed in the world. No fewer than four have received the Nobel Prize for Literature – W B Yeats, George Bernard Shaw, Samuel Becket and Seamus Heaney. Many consider it surprising that Dubliner James Joyce did not receive the same recognition. Other Irish writers include Jonathan Swift, Oliver Goldsmith, Richard Brinsley Sheridan and Oscar Wilde – and Bram Stoker, creator of Dracula, was born and raised in Dublin.

A bronze statue of James Joyce watches over the junction of O'Connell and Earl Streets in Dublin.

Top Ten

Above: *Jaunting car at Muckross Estate*
Right: *Cross at the sacred site of Clonmacnoise*

1
The Aran Islands

✚ 62A2

🚌 No public transport on the islands

✈ Aer Arann (☎ 091-68903) operates flights taking 6 mins from Connemara Airport, Co Galway with a capacity of 9 passengers. Mar–Oct four flights daily; Nov–Feb two flights daily

⛴ Aran Ferries Teo (☎ 091-68903) operates the Aran Flyer, a 20-min crossing from Rossaveal, Co Galway

Aran's Heritage Centre

✉ Kilronan

☎ 099-61355

🕐 Apr–Oct, daily 10–7

✋ Free

The bleak Inis Mór coastline

Bleak and virtually treeless, these three remote islands on the very edge of Europe have a fascinating cultural heritage.

From the mainland, the distant sight of the three Aran Islands is mysterious and inviting. The west coast of Ireland may seem a remote outpost of Europe, and yet here is something beyond – a place where Gaelic is still the first language, where old traditions live on and where a small population still scratch a living from the often inhospitable land. The influx of summer visitors is an important part of the economy, along with the sale of Aran knitwear.

Of the three islands – Inis Mór (Inishmore), Inis Meáin (Inishmaan) and Inis Oírr (Inisheer) – Inis Mór is the largest, and Kilronan is its main settlement. **Aran's Heritage Centre**, with exhibitions, crafts and audio-visual show, will steer you towards the many attractions of the islands, from their wonderful beaches to the plentiful historic sites.

There is evidence of prehistoric settlement on the islands. Inis Mór has no less than five stone forts, including the dramatic Dún Aonghasa, perched above a 91-m drop to the sea, and Dún Eochla on the island's highest point.

More atmospheric still are the early Christian sites. The islands have a number of ancient churches, including Teampall Bheanáin, which was built in the 6th century, and Teampall Chiaráin, dating from the 8th or 9th centuries.

The islands deserve more than just a day trip, which can only scratch the surface of what they have to offer.

2
Brugh Na Boinne

The valley of the River Boyne east of Slane is a remarkable area containing evidence of Ireland's most ancient history.

This great neolithic cemetery consists of at least 40 burial sites, and the landscape is dotted with standing stones and earthworks, but the crowning glory is the great passage grave at **Newgrange**. Older than Stonehenge, it is a mound of enormous dimen-

Ancient spiral carvings at the tomb entrance

sions, 11m high and 90m across with a glittering white quartzite retaining wall encircled with large kerbstones at its base, and these are incised with geometric patterns. Beyond this are the 12 surviving stones of a great circle that originally stretched all the way around the mound.

The entrance to the tomb is marked by a massive stone with triple spiral ornamentations, and above it is an opening through which the rays of the rising sun illuminate the interior of the central chamber for about 15 minutes on just one day of the year – the winter solstice, 21 December (the phenomenon is re-created with artificial light the rest of the year, at the end of the guided tour).

Inside the chamber it is possible to see the intricate construction of the roof, which still keeps out water after about 5,000 years, and the recesses into which the remains of the cremated dead were placed, together with final offerings. And there are more of the mysterious geometric patterns on the stones. Much about Newgrange remains a mystery, but there is an interpretive centre at the site which explains what has been discovered.

Try to visit Newgrange outside the peak summer season, when it can get uncomfortably crowded, with lengthy queues for the guided tour, and around the winter solstice, when it is almost impossible to get in. People book years in advance to witness the illumination of the chamber on that morning.

The other major sites of Brugh Na Boinne are the two burial chambers at **Knowth**, northwest of Slane, and the larger but less acessible site at Dowth, to the northeast of the town.

Newgrange and Knowth

✠ 31C5

✉ Donore

☎ 041-24488

🕐 Mar–Apr, daily 9:30–5:30; May, late Sep 9–6:30; Jun–mid-Sep 9–7; Oct 9:30–5:30; Nov–Feb 9:30–5; Closed 23–7 Dec

🍴 Coffee shop (£)

♿ Good

🖐 Moderate

3
Clonmacnoise

✝ 63C2

✉ Clonfanlough,
Shannonbridge

☎ 0905-74195

🕐 Mid-Mar–May & mid-
Sep–Oct, daily 10–6;
Jun–mid-Sep, daily, 9–7;
Nov–mid-Mar, daily
10–5; Closed 25 Dec

🍴 Coffee shop in summer
(£)

♿ Few

✊ Moderate

*One of Clonmacnoise's
well-preserved round
towers*

*One of the most atmospheric places in Ireland,
this ancient monastic city stands in
peaceful seclusion beside the River Shannon.*

In AD 545 St Ciaran (or Kieran) founded a monastery in this
isolated place, cut off from the rest of Ireland by the wide
River Shannon and surrounding bogland, and accessible
only by boat. In this remote location his monastery grew
into an ecclesiastical city, the most important religious
foundation of its time in Ireland, and as his burial site it
became a place of pilgrimage.

Over the ensuing centuries more and more buildings
were added, and the ruins we see today are the most
extensive of their kind in the country, including a cathedral,
eight churches which were built between the 10th and
13th centuries, two round towers, three high crosses, 200
early Christian grave slabs, two holy wells and a
13th-century castle. A short way distant is the beautiful
Romanesque 'Nun's Church', which was built
by Devorgilla, wife of chieftain
Tiernan O'Rourke. It was
her abduction by Dermot
MacMurrough, King of
Leinster, that led to conflict
which resulted in the Anglo-
Norman invasion of Ireland.

Clonmacnoise was also the
burial place of the Kings of
Connaught and of Tara,
including the last High King of
Ireland, Rory O'Conor, who
was laid to rest here in 1198.

In spite of the remoteness
of its setting, Clonmacnoise
was known throughout Europe
as a centre of excellence in art
and literature. Masterpieces of
Irish craftsmanship and
intricate decoration produced
here include the gold and
silver Crozier of Clonmacnoise
and the Cross of Cong, now in
the Treasury of the National
Museum in Dublin (▶ 24), and
the earliest known manuscript
in the vernacular Irish, the
Book of the Dun Cow, was
produced here.

4
The Dingle

*Of all the glories of the west coast,
the Dingle Peninsula is the most beautiful and
the most dramatic.*

The Dingle has many attractions, but best of all is its wonderful coastal scenery. Along the north coast are great sweeping bays, backed by huge brooding mountains; the south has pretty little coves and the lovely Inch beach, and in the west is the incomparable sight of the Blasket Islands off Slea Head. After exploring the coast, the drive across the Connor Pass north from Dingle and over Mount Brandon opens up a whole new perspective, with magnificent views down towards Brandon Bay.

Dingle is the main centre, a delightful town of well-maintained, brightly painted houses and shops with a

✚ 48A2

🛈 Dingle Tourist Office: Main Street (☎ 066 51188)

🚢 Dingle Bay Ferries (☎ 066-51640), operate scenic one-hour boat trips around the Bay (Apr–Oct)

❓ Dingle Way long-distance footpath, 49.6km between Dingle and Tralee; Dingle Regatta in Aug

picturesque harbour which still supports a working fishing fleet as well as pleasure craft. These include boat trips to see the famous friendly dolphin, Fungi, who lives near the harbour mouth. Dingle has catered for tourists without being swamped by them, and is a lively place with an annual cultural festival and a famous regatta.

Ancient sites on The Dingle include a cliff-top Iron-Age fort near Ventry, Minard Castle, above Dingle Bay, and Gallarus Oratory, a tiny church dating from around the 8th century, between Ballyferriter and Ballynana. Nearby Kilmalkedar Church, dating from the 12th century, contains the Alphabet Stone, inscribed with both Roman and ancient Irish characters.

The Irish style of house painting is beautifully demonstrated in this Dingle street

19

5
The Giant's Causeway

75C3 (general area)

172 Ballycastle–
Portrush; summer
services 177 from
Coleraine and 252 from
Belfast and Larne

Portrush (11km)

Causeway Visitor Centre

44 Causeway Road,
Bushmills

012657 31855

Mar–Jun daily; Sep
10–5; Jul–Aug, daily
10–7; Oct–Feb, daily
10–4:30

Tea room (£)

Good

Free. Moderate charge
for car park and extra
charge for audio-visual
theatre

*This unique geological phenomenon,
set on a coastline of outstanding beauty, is one of
the wonders of the natural world.*

About 40,000 columns of basalt cluster on the shoreline
here, forming stepping stones from these cliffs down into
the water. Most of them are hexagonal, but some have
four, five, seven or eight sides, and the tallest rise to
around 12m. The only other place in the world where such
columns can be seen is on Staffa, an island off the coast of
Scotland, and this is simply because they are part of the
same formation. Little wonder, then, that the Causeway
has been designated a World Heritage Site.

The columns are the result of volcanic action some 60
million years ago, which caused molten basalt to seep up
through the chalky bedrock. When it cooled, the rock
crystalised into these regular formations, but it would be
easy to believe that the blocks were stacked by some
giant hand, driven on in its monumental task by the force
of some great purpose.

This, of course, is what the ancient Irish believed to be
the case, and who else could have completed the task but
the legendary giant Finn McCool, the Ulster warrior who
was said to inhabit this Antrim headland. When he once

scooped up a clod of earth to throw at a rival, the place he scooped it from filled with water to become Lough Neagh, the largest lake in the British Isles, and the clod landed in the Irish sea and became the Isle of Man. In the story of the causeway, he built it so that he could cross the sea to reach the lady giant of his dreams, who lived on Staffa – a tall story in more ways than one.

The reality is equally remarkable, but whatever created the causeway, it is a magnificent sight, particularly when approached on foot from above. There is a cliff-top path all along this stretch of coastline, which can be joined at Blackrock, 2.5km from Causeway Head, or from the **Causeway Visitor Centre**.

The Visitor Centre is on the cliff top, leaving the causeway in splendid isolation, and is a good introduction to the site. It includes an audio-visual theatre, where a 25-minute show tells the story of the formation of the causeway. There is also an exhibition area with displays including birdlife and the legend of Finn McCool. A mini-bus runs from here to the causeway at regular intervals throughout the summer and guided tours are available.

Beside the centre is the **Causeway School Museum**, a reconstructed 1920s schoolroom complete with learning aids and toys of the era.

Causeway School Museum

 Causeway Road, Bushmills

 012657 31053

 Jul–Aug, daily 11–5

Good

Cheap

Sunlight and shadows emphasise the geometric shapes of the Causeway

6
Kilkenny

✝ 31A2

🚆 Kilkenny 1.5km

Cityscope Exhibition

✉ Rose Inn Street

☎ 056-21755

🕐 May–Sep, Mon–Sat 9–6,
Sun 10–4:30; Oct–Apr,
Tue–Sat 9–5:15; Sun
9–12:45, 2–5:15

♿ Few

✋ Moderate

Kilkenny Castle

✉ City centre

☎ 056-21450

🕐 Jun–Sep, Tue–Sun 10–7;
Apr–May, Tue–Sun
10:30–5; Oct–Mar,
Tue–Sat 10:30–12:45,
2–5, Sun 11–12:45, 2–5.
Closed Mon

🍴 Coffee shop Jun–Sep (£)

♿ Few

✋ Moderate

*The richly-coloured walls
of Kilkenny Castle's Long
Gallery are hung with fine
works of art*

*Narrow medieval streets and alleys linking the
great castle and cathedral bear witness to
Kilkenny's rich history and architectural heritage.*

Standing on a bend of the River Nore, Kilkenny is one of
Ireland's most beautiful towns, with delightful little streets
to explore, high quality craft studios, good restaurants and
an exceptional range of historic buildings. The **Cityscope
Exhibition**, housed in the 16th-century Shee Alms House,
includes a fascinating scale model of the town in its 17th-
century heyday.

In medieval times, the town rivalled Dublin in importance and the great **castle** here was the stronghold of the
most powerful family in Ireland at the time, the Butlers,
Earls and Dukes of Ormonde. Though its origins are back
in Norman times, the castle was adapted over the
centuries and now reflects the splendour of the 1830s,
enhanced by the National Furniture Collection and a fine art
gallery in the former servants' quarters.

Opposite the castle is the Kilkenny Design Centre,
which was established in the 1960s to bring Irish craftsmanship to new heights of excellence. Not only was the
centre resoundingly successful, it became the spearhead
of a crafts revival that has attracted many fine craft
workers from all over the world to the county.

Kilkenny originally grew up around the 6th-century
monastery founded by St Canice, to whom the cathedral is
dedicated. Built on the site of the original monastery, it
remains one of the finest 13th-century buildings in Ireland,
in spite of the fact that Cromwell used it as a stable in
1650, and contains impressive monuments of black
Kilkenny marble. Beside the cathedral is the well-
preserved round tower of the original monastery, which
gives wonderful views over this remarkable city.

7
Muckross House

Among Ireland's foremost stately homes, Muckross has folk and farm museums and beautiful gardens – all within the Killarney National Park.

When Henry Arthur Herbert, MP for Co Kerry, built his Elizabethan-style mansion in 1843, he could not have found a more perfect site, looking out towards Muckross Lake and surrounded by wonderful scenery that was destined to become a National Park. It has elegant rooms, with grand portraits, glittering Venetian mirrors and Chippendale furniture, and visitors can reflect on the good fortune of one Maud Bowers Bourne, who was given the house as a wedding present in 1911. Her family presented the house and estate to the Irish nation in 1932 in her memory.

While the house sums up the lifestyle of the landed gentry in Victorian times, the servants' quarters have been converted into a museum of Kerry folk life, with displays and craft workshops. Out in the grounds, a 28-hectare farm has been constructed to demonstrate farming methods which were used before mechanisation. The rare Kerry cow, a small, black, hardy animal, is being bred here in order to save the herd from extinction.

The gardens at Muckross are renowned for their beauty, and are particularly colourful in early summer when the rhododendrons and azaleas are flowering. Many tender and exotic species thrive in the mild climate, and there are lovely water and rock gardens. A number of nature trails of various lengths begin here, from a one-hour stroll to a 16-km circular Heritage Trail through the most extensive natural yew woods in Europe, which can be walked, cycled (bicycles for hire) or travelled in a horse-drawn jaunting car.

✚ 48B2

✉ 5km south of Killarney

☎ 064-31440

🕓 Mar–Jun, daily 9–6; Jul–Aug, daily 9–7; Sep–Mar, daily 9–5:30

🍴 Cafe (£)

🚌 From Killarney

♿ Few

✋ Moderate

❓ Special horse-drawn jaunting cars from Killarney to house

Beautifully proportioned Muckross House illustrates the lives of the rich landowner and the working artisan

8
The National Museum, Dublin

✝ 37C2

✉ Kildare Street, Merrion Row and Merrion Street, Dublin 2

☎ 01-6777444

🕐 Tue–Sat 10–5, Sun 2–5. Closed Mon, 25 Dec and Good Fri

🍴 Coffee shop (£)

🚌 10, 11, 13 from O'Connell Street

🚆 Pearse station 5-minutes walk

♿ Few

✋ Free

❓ Guided tours (Jun–Sep) cheap

A magnificent collection of ancient gold objects and the finest masterpieces of Irish Celtic art are among the treasures here.

In a fine building on Kildare Street, the National Museum of Ireland is a wonderful place to wander among collections which span the ages from 2000 BC to the 20th century. Beyond the great circular entrance hall, pride of place goes to the museum's glittering collection of ancient gold, where hundreds of items such as collars, bracelets, dress fasteners, ear-rings and hair ornaments dating from about 2200 to 700 BC are displayed in climate-controlled glass cases. One of the collars, dating from 700 BC was discovered by a farm boy near the Gleninsheen wedge tomb in The Burren in Co Clare.

Some of the gold bears faint traces of Celtic decoration, but the best examples of this are to be found in The National Treasury. Intricate Celtic patterns are still much in favour today, particularly on jewellery, but there is nothing to compare with the delicate intricacy of the workmanship to be seen here. Some of the patterns worked in silver and gold many centuries ago are almost too tiny to be appreciated by the naked eye. The greatest treasures include the Tara Brooch, probably the most important and the most copied of all the Celtic jewels, the Cross of Cong, the Ardagh Chalice and St Patrick's Bell.

Viking Age Ireland is the most extensive exhibition ever to deal with the time of the first Dubliners, from around 800 to 1150, with a huge variety of artefacts from Wood Quay and other sites in the city. There are ornate swords, intricate jewellery and a wealth of the ordinary implements of every-day life. *Ar Thóir na Saoirse* (The Road to Independence) is an evocative telling of the events of 1916 to 1923, including the Easter Rising and the Civil War. The upper floors of the museum include collections of porcelain, glass and scientific instruments and a music room with a fine collection of Irish harps and uilleann pipes.

The 8th-century Ardagh Chalice represents a triumph of Celtic art and craftsmanship

9
The Rock of Cashel

Ancient seat of the Kings of Munster and medieval religious centre, the Rock of Cashel is an awe-inspiring sight.

This single craggy hill, rising out of the surrounding plain and topped by a cluster of wonderful medieval buildings, dominates the skyline. It is a great landmark which draws more than the eye – its romantic outline of ruined towers and graceful arches seems to beckon from a distance.

The great rock was the obvious choice as the fortress of the Kings of Munster, who ruled the southern part of Ireland, and Cashel came to prominence in the 4th or 5th century AD. Legend has it that St Patrick came here to baptise the king, and that during the ceremony, the saint accidentally drove the sharp end of his crozier through the king's foot. The king bore the pain unflinchingly because he believed it to be part of the initiation.

✚ 49C2

✉ Rock of Cashel

☎ 062-61437

◆ Mid-Mar–mid-Jun, daily 9:30–5:30; mid-Jun–mid-Sep, daily 9–7:30; mid-Sep–mid-Mar, daily 9:30–4:30

🚌 Dublin–Cork buses

♿ Few

✋ Moderate

❓ Guided tours on request

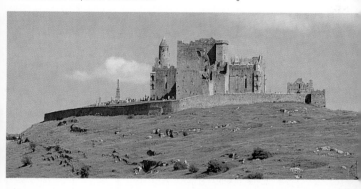

The dominant building on the rock is the 13th-century St Patrick's Cathedral, roofless now, but still impressive, with its long nave and chancel and a 26-m tower. Inside are a wealth of monuments, including important tombs, and the west end is formed by a 15th-century castle, built as the Archbishop's residence.

The Round Tower and Cormac's Chapel are the oldest structures on the Rock, dating from the 11th to 12th centuries, and the chapel contains a remarkable stone sarcophagus carved with sophisticated Celtic patterns.

One of the later buildings, the 15th-century Hall of the Vicars, is one of the first you see on the Rock, with a display of stone carvings in its vaulted undercroft and above it a splendid hall with a minstrels' gallery, huge fireplace and wonderful timbered ceiling.

Tantalising glimpses of the Rock of Cashel from the approach roads are a stirring sight

10
Ulster American Folk Park

The lives and experiences of Ulster emigrants to the New World are authentically re-created at this splendid open-air museum.

 74B2

 2 Mellon Road, Castletown

 01662-243292

Easter–Sep, Mon–Sat 11–6:30, Sun and public hols 11:30–7; Oct–Easter, Mon–Fri 10:30–5

 Cafe (£)

273 Belfast–Londonderry

Good

Moderate

 Special events to celebrate the Ulster-American connection are held throughout the year

This was the face of a new life in the New World for many Ulster emigrants

In a great tide of emigration during the 18th and 19th centuries over 2 million people left Ulster for a different life in the New World. Among them was five-year-old Thomas Mellon, who went on to become a judge and founder of the Pittsburg dynasty of bankers, and it is around his childhood home that this museum has been created. Buildings have been reconstructed on the site, giving a complete picture of the world that the emigrants left behind and the one that was awaiting them on the other side of the Atlantic.

The Ulster section includes a typical one-room cottage of the late 18th century, a forge and weaver's cottage, schoolhouse and post office, places of worship and a 19th-century street of shops, with original Victorian shopfronts. Houses include the boyhood homes of John Joseph Hughes, the first Roman Catholic Archbishop of New York and Robert Campbell, who became a fur trader in the Rockies and a successful merchant in St Louis.

On the dockside, visitors can see a typical merchant's office and a boarding house, where emigrants would await their sailing, then board a reconstruction of the kind of sailing ship which carried them to their new lives.

Beyond this you emerge into the American section of the park, with log houses and barns, including a replica of the six-roomed farmhouse that Thomas Mellon's father built. The buildings contain over 2,000 19th-century artefacts collected in Pennsylvania and Virginia.

What To See

Above: *Garinish Point, Beara Peninsula*
Right: *Kinsale local*

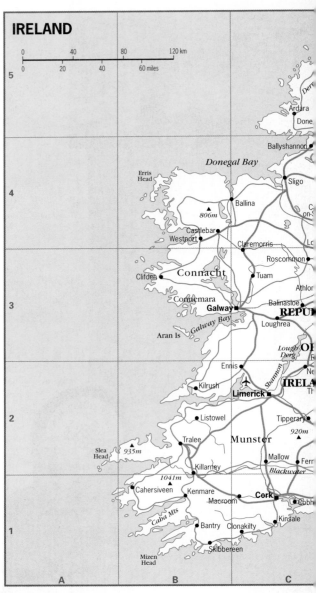

IRELAND

0   40   80   120 km
0 20   40   60 miles

5

Derr
Ardara
Done
Ballyshannon

Donegal Bay
Erris
Head
Sligo

4
▲ 806m
Ballina
C
on-
Castlebar
Westport
Claremorris
Lc
Roscommon

Clifden
Connacht
Tuam
Athlor

3
Connemara
Balinasloe
REPU
Galway
Loughrea
OF
Galway Bay
Aran Is
Lough
Derg
F
Ennis
Shannon
Ne
IRELA
Kilrush
✈
Th
Limerick

2
Listowel
Tipperary
Tralee
Munster
920m
Slea
Head
▲ 935m
Mallow ▲ Ferr
Killarney
Blackwater
▲ 1041m
Cahersiveen
Kenmare
Cork
Macroom
Cbbh
Caha Mts
Kinsale
1
Bantry   Clonakilty
Mizen
Head
Skibbereen

A   B   C

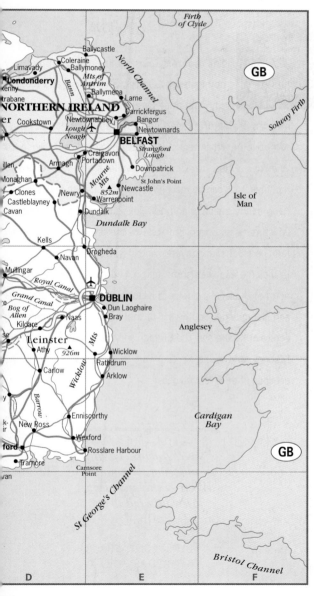

Firth
of Clyde

Ballycastle

Coleraine
Limavady   Ballymoney

Londonderry   *Mts of Antrim*
Kenny
trabane   Ballymena

NORTHERN IRELAND   Larne

er   Cookstown   Newtownabbey   Carrickfergus
Lough Neagh   Bangor
Newtownards

BELFAST

illen   Armagh   Craigavon   *Strangford Lough*
Portadown

Monaghan   *Mourne Mts*   Downpatrick
St John's Point
Clones   Newry   ▲852m   Newcastle
Castleblayney   Warrenpoint
Cavan
Dundalk

Dundalk Bay

Kells

Navan   Drogheda

Mullingar

Royal Canal

Grand Canal
e
Bog of Allen   **DUBLIN**
Kildare   Naas   Dun Laoghaire
Bray
se
Leinster   *Wicklow Mts*
Athy   ▲926m   Wicklow
Rathdrum
Carlow   Arklow

Barrow

y
New Ross   Enniscorthy
k-ir
Wexford
ford   Rosslare Harbour

Tramore
van   Carnsore Point

GB

North Channel

Solway Firth

Isle of
Man

Anglesey

Cardigan
Bay

GB

St George's Channel

Bristol Channel

D   E   F

29

The East

The eastern part of Ireland is inevitably dominated by Dublin, a charming and elegant city with a lot to see and do, but the east has much more to offer than just the capital. Ireland's most extensive mountain region is just to the south of Dublin in Co Wicklow, where remote, silent valleys and wild exposed mountain tops can be reached in less than half an hour's drive.

Long sandy beaches and golf links stretch along the coast, which remains unspoilt in spite of the presence of the main ferry ports. The resorts retain an old-fashioned appeal.

Inland, the east has some fascinating places to see. To the north of Dublin is a cluster of historic sites including Tara, Kells and Newgrange. Southwest of the capital is the horse-racing centre of Kildare and The Curragh and the wonderful old city of Kilkenny, and in the far south are the pretty villages and fine beaches of the Wexford coast.

'Sweet Auburn, loveliest village of the plain, Where health and plenty cheered the labouring swain.'

OLIVER GOLDSMITH
The Deserted Village (1770)

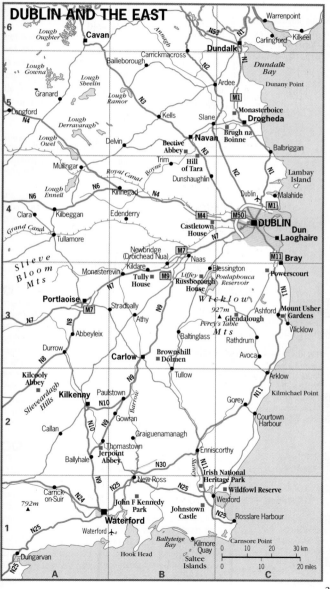

DUBLIN AND THE EAST

Warrenpoint
Carlingford
Kilkeel

Cavan
Lough Oughter
6

Lough Gowna
Bailieborough
Carrickmacross
Dundalk
N53
N1

Dundalk Bay
Dunany Point

Lough Sheelin
Granard
Lough Ramor
N2
Ardee

5
Longford
N4
Lough Derravaragh
N3
Kells
Slane
M1
Monasterboice
Drogheda

Lough Owel
Delvin
Bective Abbey
Navan
Brugh na Boinne
Balbriggan

Mullingar
Royal Canal
Boyne
Trim
Hill of Tara
N3
N2
N1
Lambay Island

N6
Lough Ennell
N6
Kinnegad
N4
Dunshaughlin
Dublin ✈
Malahide

4
Clara
Kilbeggan
Edenderry
M4
M50
M1
DUBLIN
Dun Laoghaire

Tullamore
Grand Canal
Castletown House
N7
M11
Bray

Slieve Bloom Mts
Monasterevin
Newbridge (Droichead Nua)
Naas
M7
Blessington
Powerscourt

Portlaoise
M7
N7
Kildare
Tully House
M9
Liffey
Russborough House
Poulaphouca Reservoir
N11

3
N7
N8
Stradbally
N9
Wicklow
927m ▲
Percy's Table
Glendalough
Ashford
Mount Usher Gardens

Abbeyleix
Athy
Mts
Rathdrum
Wicklow

Durrow
N8
Baltinglass
Avoca

Kilcooly Abbey
Carlow
Brownshill Dolmen
Tullow
Arklow
Kilmichael Point

2
Slieveardagh Hills
Kilkenny
Paulstown
N10
Barrow
N9
Gorey
N11
Courtown Harbour

Callan
N10
Gowran
Graiguenamanagh
Enniscorthy
Irish National Heritage Park

Ballyhale
Jerpoint Abbey
Thomastown
N30
Slaney
N11
Wildfowl Reserve

Carrick-on-Suir
792m ▲
N24
N9
New Ross
N25
Johnstown Castle
Wexford
Rosslare Harbour

1
N25
Waterford
John F Kennedy Park
N25
N25

Dungarvan
N25
Waterford ✈
Ballyteige Bay
Kilmore Quay
Saltee Islands
Hook Head
Carnsore Point

0   10   20   30 km
0   10   20 miles

A   B   C

Massive medieval walls give no hint of the sumptuous 18th-century interiors of Dublin Castle

Dublin

Part of Dublin's charm is that it only takes a few days of wandering around its attractive streets and leafy squares – and into its atmospheric pubs – to feel that you know the city intimately. And yet, every visit reveals some new delight. Above all, Dublin lacks that all-consuming sense of urgency that can make other capitals so tiring.

Dublin has everything a capital city should have – magnificent architecture, excellent shopping, lively entertainments and cultural events, superb museums and galleries, colourful parks and gardens and a strong sense of history, and it is bordered by the Wicklow Mountains.

The city is over 1,000 years old, and its castle and cathedrals were built by the Anglo-Normans who arrived in the 12th century. But the enduring image of Dublin is of the Georgian era, because so many of the splendid terraces and town houses have been well preserved.

What to See in Dublin

BANK OF IRELAND

In 1800 the Irish Parliament voted itself out of existence by the Act of Union. The redundant Parliament House, a magnificent classical building, was soon acquired by the Bank of Ireland for their headquarters. Despite internal alterations, the House of Lords remains with 18th-century tapestries. The bank now has a modern headquarters in Baggot Street, but they welcome visitors to their old building during banking hours. The Foster Place entrance leads to the Bank of Ireland Arts Centre, which hosts a variety of events and includes the Story of Banking, an interactive museum of banking and Irish history.

37C3
Bank of Ireland Arts Centre: Foster Place
01-6711488
Tue–Fri 10–4, Sat 2–5, Sun 10–1. Tours of House of Lords: Tue 10:30, 11:30, 1:45. Closed bank hols
Coffee shop (£)
All city centre buses
Good Cheap

DUBLIN CASTLE

Soon after the Anglo-Normans arrived in Ireland in the 12th century, King John ordered the building of Dublin Castle and it remained the centre of English power in Ireland until 1922. In spite of its great medieval walls and round bastions, much of the castle is a product of the 18th century, including the splendid State Apartments, where presidents are inaugurated and visiting dignatories received. The Chester Beatty Library, one of the world's best collections of Oriental and European manuscripts, was due to take up residence within the castle in 1997; telephone to confirm its arrival.

36B3
Dame Street
01-6777129
Mon–Fri 10–5, Sat, Sun, bank hols, 2–5 (subject to alteration at short notice)
Self-service restaurant (£)
50, 50a, 56a, 77 & 77a (Eden Quay) 77b (Aston Quay)
Few Cheap

DUBLINIA ✪

Developed by the Medieval Trust, Dublinia tells the story of the city from the arrival of the Anglo-Normans in the 12th century until the closure of the monasteries in 1540. It is housed in a beautifully preserved old building, the former Synod Hall, linked to Christ Church Cathedral by an ancient covered bridge, and includes historical tableaux which are interpreted by a personal cassette commentary. There is also an audio-visual presentation, a model of medieval Dublin, and a collection of artefacts from the National Museum.

DUBLIN'S VIKING ADVENTURE ✪✪

Over 1,000 years ago Dublin was a Viking city and, in the area where they had their settlement, this entertaining attraction has recreated the day-to-day life of the Norse settlers. Visitors can stroll through their narrow streets, visit their homes and workplaces and chat to the 'Vikings'. More than just a themed 'experience', the Viking town is based on information revealed from local excavations, and there is an extensive exhibition of the artefacts that were unearthed. Entertaining Viking-style banquets are held here in the evenings.

DUBLIN WRITERS' MUSEUM ✪

No other city in the world has spawned so many writers of international repute, including four Nobel prize winners, and this museum is a celebration of that literary heritage. The displays, in the magnificent surroundings of a restored 18th-century mansion, encompass the whole spectrum of Irish works, from the 8th-century *Book of Kells* to the present, taking in Swift, Sheridan, Shaw, Wilde, Yeats, Joyce and Beckett along the way. One room is devoted entirely to children's literature, and there are regular exhibitions and readings.

✚ 36B3
✉ St Michael's Hill, Christ Church
☎ 01-6794611
🕐 Apr–Sep, daily 10–5; Oct–Mar, Mon–Sat 11–4, Sun & bank hol; 10–4:30. Closed 24–6 Dec
🍴 Coffee Shop (£)
🚌 50 (Eden Quay), 78a (Aston Quay)
♿ Few 🔳 Expensive

✉ Essex Street West, Temple Bar
☎ 01-6796040
🕐 Weekdays 10–4:30, Sun & public hols 11:30– 5:30. Closed Tue & Wed
🍴 Coffee shop) (£)
🚌 78a & 79 from Aston Quay
🚇 DART Tara Street
♿ Good 🔳 Expensive

✚ 36B5
✉ 18 Parnell Square North
☎ 01-8722077
🕐 Mon–Sat 10–5, Sun & public hols 11:30–6
🍴 Restaurant (£££) and coffee shop (£)
🚌 All city centre buses
🚇 DART Tara Street
♿ Few 🔳 Moderate

GUINNESS HOP STORE

Guinness, one of the most potent symbols of Irishness, is now brewed all over the world, at a rate of 10 million glasses a day – and this is where it all started, when Arthur Guinness purchased the premises in 1759 and began brewing the 'black stuff'. The Guinness Hop Store on Crane Street now houses the 'World of Guinness Exhibition', with entertaining displays and an audio-visual show about the history and manufacture of Dublin's most famous product. Visitors get an introduction to brewing by walking through a reconstructed Victorian mash tun, and there is a very pleasant bar in which to sample the brew.

🚩 36A3
✉ St James's Gate
☎ 01-4536700
🕓 Apr–Sep, Mon–Sat 9:30–5, Sun & bank hols 10:30–4:30; Oct–Mar, Mon–Sat 9:30–4, Sun & bank hols 12–4
🍴 Coffee shop (£)
🚌 78a & 68a from Aston Quay; 123 from O'Connell Street
🚆 DART Tara Street
♿ Few 🔆 Moderate

HUGH LANE MUNICIPAL GALLERY OF MODERN ART

Founded in 1908, this was the first public gallery of modern art in Ireland, and is now the second-largest collection in the country. In 1993 it was moved to this lovely Georgian Mansion, a fine setting for works from the Irish, French and British schools. The impressionists are well represented, with works by Manet, Monet, Degas and Renoir, and there is a Stained Glass Room, with examples by Harry Clarke, Wilhelmina Geddes, Evie Hone and James Scanlon. On Sundays there are concerts and public lectures.

🚩 36B4
✉ Charlemont House, Parnell Square
☎ 01-8741903
🕓 Tue–Fri 9:30–6, Sat 9:30–5, Sun 11–5. Closed Mon
🍴 Restaurant (££)
🚌 All city centre buses
🚆 DART Connolly
♿ Good
🔆 Free

NATIONAL GALLERY OF IRELAND

First opened in 1864, this wonderful gallery has one of the finest collections of European art in the world. Displayed in one of Dublin's most splendid Georgian buildings, the gallery contains nearly 2,500 paintings, over 5,000 drawings, watercolours and miniatures, over 3,000 prints and more than 300 pieces of sculpture and *objets d'art*. An extensive collection of Irish art is on permanent display, and every major European School of Painting is represented.

🚩 37C2
✉ Merrion Square West
☎ 01-6615133
🕓 Mon–Sat 10–5:30 (8:30 on Thu), Sun 2–5. Closed Good Fri, 24–6 Dec
🍴 Self-service restaurant (£)
🚌 5, 7, 7A (Burgh Quay), 10 (O'Connell Street) 44, 47
🚆 DART Pearse
♿ Good 🔆 Free

NATIONAL LIBRARY

The National Library houses the nation's greatest archive of books, over half a million, including some first editions. There are also manuscripts, maps, prints and drawings, newspapers, letters of well-known Irish literary figures and microfilm copies of Irish manuscripts and documents which are stored abroad. Tickets are issued for reading the books. Changing exhibitions are regularly held in the entrance hall.

🚩 37C2
✉ Kildare Street
☎ 01-6618811
🕓 Mon 10–9, Tue–Wed 2–9, Thu–Fri 10–5, Sat 10–1. Closed 4 weeks each year
🚌 10, 11, 13 from O'Connell Street
🚆 DART Pearse
♿ Few 🔆 Free

NATIONAL MUSEUM (▶ 24, TOP TEN)

TRINITY COLLEGE ✪✪✪

Through the Palladian façade of Trinity College is not only an oasis of peace and quiet in the heart of the busy city centre, but also one of its finest ranges of buildings. The college was founded in 1592 by Elizabeth I, with many fine buildings from the 18th and 19th centuries. The finest of them all is the great **Library**, which contains some of Ireland's greatest treasures. Magnificent illuminated manuscripts on display include the 9th-century *Book of Kells* and the *Book of Armagh*. Also within the college is the **Dublin Experience**, a multi-media show telling the story of Dublin and its people.

✚ 37C3

Library
* College Green
* 01-6082308
* All year, Mon–Sat 9:30–5, Sun 12–4:30. Closed 10 days at Christmas
* All city centre buses
* Good
* Moderate

Dublin Experience
* College Green
* 01-6081177
* Mid-May–Sep, daily 10–5
* Coffee shop (£)
* All city centre buses
* Good
* Moderate

Stacked to its wonderful barrel-vaulted ceiling with ancient volumes, Trinity College Library, an architectural as well as a literary treasurehouse

*The Bank of Ireland on
College Green*

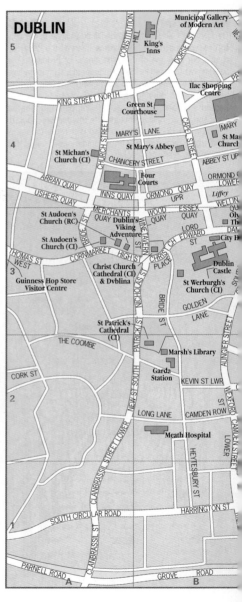

DUBLIN

5

Municipal Gallery
of Modern Art

King's
Inns

CONSTITUTION HILL

DORSET ST

WE

Ilac Shopping
Centre

PA

KING STREET NORTH

Green St
Courthouse

MARY'S LANE

St Mary's Abbey

CAPEL STREET

MARY

St Ma
Church

4

St Michan's
Church (CI)

CHURCH STREET

CHANCERY STREET

ABBEY ST UP

ARRAN QUAY

Four
Courts

ORMOND
LOWER

INNS QUAY

ORMOND QUAY
UPR

Liffey

USHERS QUAY

MERCHANTS
QUAY

WOOD
QUAY

ESSEX
QUAY

WELLIN
QU

St Audoen's
Church (RC)

Dublin's
Viking
Adventure

WINE TAVERN ST

Oly
The

BRIDE ST

St Audoen's
Church (CI)

LORD
EDWARD
ST

DAM

City H

THOMAS ST
WEST

CORNMARKET

HIGH ST

NICHOLAS ST

CHRIST CH
PLACE

Dublin
Castle

3

Guinness Hop Store
Visitor Centre

Christ Church
Cathedral (CI)
& Dvblina

St Werburgh's
Church (CI)

GOLDEN
LANE

BRIDE ST

THE COOMBE

St Patrick's
Cathedral
(CI)

PATRICK'S ST

Marsh's Library

AUNGIER STREET

CORK ST

Garda
Station

KEVIN ST LWR

WEXFORD ST

2

NEW ST SOUTH

LONG LANE

CAMDEN ROW

CAMDEN STREET LOWER

Meath Hospital

CLANBRASSIL STREET LOWER

HEYTESBURY ST

1

SOUTH CIRCULAR ROAD

HARRINGTON ST

PARNELL ROAD

CLANBRASSIL ST

GROVE ROAD

A

B

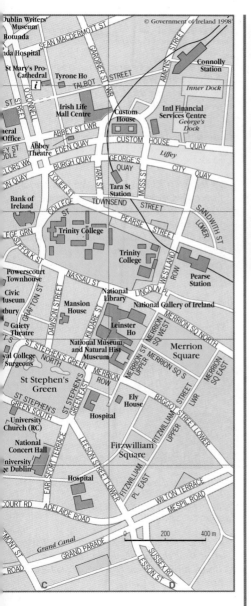

© Government of Ireland 1998

Dublin Writers' Museum

Rotunda

...da Hospital

St Mary's Pro-Cathedral

Tyrone Ho

Irish Life Mall Centre

Custom House

Connolly Station

Inner Dock

Intl Financial Services Centre
George's Dock

...neral Office

Abbey Theatre

Custom House Quay

Eden Quay

Liffey

George's Quay

City Quay

Tara St Station

Bank of Ireland

Townsend Street

Sandwith St Lower

College Grn

Trinity College

Pearse Street

Suffolk St

Powerscourt Townhouse

Trinity College

Civic Museum

Nassau St

Westland Row

Pearse Station

Mansion House

National Library

Lincoln Pl

Gaiety Theatre

National Gallery of Ireland

Leinster Ho

Merrion Sq North

St Stephen's Green North

National Museum and Natural Hist Museum

Merrion Square

Royal College of Surgeons

Merrion Row

Merrion Sq East

St Stephen's Green

Ely House

Baggot Street Lower

Merrion Sq S

University Church (RC)

St Stephen's Green South

Hospital

National Concert Hall

...niversity ...ge Dublin

Fitzwilliam Square

Hospital

Fitzwilliam St Lower

Fitzwilliam Pl East

Earlsfort Terrace

Wilton Terrace

...court Rd

Adelaide Road

Mespil Road

0   200   400 m

Grand Canal

Grand Parade

Sussex Rd

Leeson St

...road

C

D

Wide O'Connell Street is Dublin's principal thoroughfare north of the Liffey

A Walk Around Dublin

Distance
About 4km

Time
3–4 hours

Start/end point
Grafton Street
✝ 37C3
🚌 All city centre buses

Lunch
Fitzsimmons Bar and
Restaurant (££)
✉ East Essex Street,
Temple Bar
☎ 01-6779315

This walk starts in Dublin's most famous shopping street,
then takes in many of the city's major attractions.

*Walk south along Grafton Street, cross the road
and enter St Stephen's Green, leaving by the
small gate on the left. Cross the road and go
forward along Kildare Street.*

The National Museum, on the right, is Ireland's treasurehouse, with some stunning objects and fascinating
exhibitions. exhibitions (▶ 24).

*At the end of Kildare Street go left into Nassau
Street, then right to reach College Green with
Trinity College on the right (▶ 35). Cross the
junction Westmoreland Street, keep forward
across O'Connell Bridge and turn left alongside
the river. Cross Halfpenny Bridge (footbridge),
then go through Merchant's Arch into Temple
Bar.*

This network of little cobbled lanes is worth exploring.

*Turn right into Essex Street East, then take the
third left into Eustace Street. At the end turn
right along Dame Street.*

Dublin Castle is on the left,
its medieval origins buried
beneath 18th-century recon-
structions which house the
truly magnificent State
Apartments including the
Throne Room (▶ 32).

*The picturesque
Ha'Penny Bridge spans
the Liffey near Temple
Bar*

Keep forward to Christ Church Cathedral.

Begun in the 12th century, beautiful Christ Church is the
foremost cathedral in Dublin.

*Go down Fishamble Street to the river. Turn
right along the south bank, and at O'Connell
Bridge turn right and keep forward to Grafton
Street.*

What to See in The East

BRUGH NA BOINNE (▶ 17, TOP TEN)

CASTLETOWN HOUSE ✪
Castletown House at Celbridge is Ireland's largest and finest Palladian country house, built in the 18th century for William Connolly, Speaker of the Irish House of Commons. The central block, modelled on an Italian palazzo, is linked to its two wings by gracefully curving colonnades.

The sumptuous interiors, including the Pompeian Gallery, are largely the inspiration of Lady Louisa Lennox, who came to the house on marriage in 1785. At its heart is a magnificent hall, with sweeping cantilevered staircase and superb plasterwork. Now the headquarters of the Irish Georgian Society, Castletown House is undergoing restoration, and may not be fully accessible.

✚ 31B4
✉ Celbridge
☎ 01-6288252
🚌 67 & 67a from Dublin
▨ Moderate

CEANNUS MOR (KELLS) ✪
In AD 804 a Columban monastery was founded at Kells by monks who had fled the Viking raids on Iona. It was to become one of the great centres of Celtic Christianity, and it was here that the magnificently decorated version of the Gospels, the *Book of Kells*, was completed. This is now a prized possession of Dublin's Trinity College Library (▶ 35) after being moved there during the Cromwellian wars, but replicas are on display in the town hall and in St Columcille's church.

The town's street pattern still reflects the circular shape of the monastery, from which only a round tower and the tiny St Columcille's House remain. The original doorway of the house was 2.4m above ground level, a defensive measure which reflected troubled times. Close to the round tower, in the churchyard are three elaborately carved stone crosses, also from the 9th century. A fourth, with 30 decorative panels, stands in Market Square, but its shaft was damaged by its one-time use as a gallows.

✚ 31B5
🕐 Always accessible
🍴 Monaghan's Lounge (£)
Carrick House, Kells
☎ 046-40100

Intricate plasterwork frames one of Castletown House's works of art

An atmosphere of peace and seclusion still surrounds the monastic remains at Glendalough

GLENDALOUGH ✪✪✪

Deep in the heart of the Wicklow Mountains (➤ 45) are the atmospheric remains of a remarkable monastic city which was founded in the 6th century by St Kevin and remained an important diocese and place of pilgrimage well into the 17th century.

Various legends surround the mysterious St Kevin. He is said to have come to Glendalough to avoid the advances of a beautiful redhead with 'unholy eyes', and that he rolled himself and his putative lover in stinging nettles to dampen their desire. He may also have hurled the lady into an icy lake to cool her ardour.

The earliest parts of the remains, accessible only by boat, are on the south side of the Upper Lake and include the reconstructed Templenaskellig and St Kevin's Bed, a small cave reached with a difficult climb.

The settlement developed mainly between the 10th and 12th centuries, when most of the buildings were erected, including St Kevin's Church an oratory called St Kevin's Kitchen, the fine 31-m round tower and the Cathedral of St Peter and St Paul. There are several other churches and monastic buildings and the ruins of a prehistoric fort, as well as numerous gravestones and crosses, including the plain granite St Kevin's Cross standing 3.5m high. The Interpretive Centre by the first car park displays many antiquities found in the valley and is the starting point of guided tours.

✚ 31C3
☎ 0404-45325
🕐 Mid-Mar–May 9:30–6;
   Jun–Aug 9–6:30;
   Sep–mid-Oct 9:30–6;
   Mid-Oct–mid-Mar 9:30–5
🚌 St Kevin's Bus from
   Dublin (☎ 01-2818119)
♿ Few
💰 Cheap

IRISH NATIONAL HERITAGE PARK ✪✪

On the River Slaney, a little way west of Wexford, is the Irish National Heritage Park, which re-creates Irish life over a period of about 9,000 years, ending with the Anglo-Norman period. No less than 14 historical sites have been re-created amidst the maturing woodland of the 14-hectare site. The trappings and paraphernalia of everyday life through the ages helps to bring it all to life, and the park successfully combines the requirements of tourism with serious historical content.

✚ 31B1
✉ Ferrycarrig
☎ 053-20733
🕐 Mid-Mar–mid-Nov, daily
   10–7
🍴 Refreshments (£)
♿ Good
💰 Moderate

JERPOINT ABBEY ✪✪

Jerpoint Abbey is one of Ireland's finest monastic ruins. The first religious house here was a Benedictine abbey, founded by MacGillapatrick, King of Ossory, around 1158, but by 1180 it had been taken over by the Cistercians. Substantial remains of buildings from the 12th to the 15th centuries tower impressively above the main road. For all its size and presence, however, what is most interesting here are the amusing carvings along the restored cloister arcade, the fine monuments and various effigies, including that of Felix O'Dulany, Bishop of Ossory (1178–1202) which stands in the chancel.

✚ 31A2
✉ Thomastown
☎ 056-24623
🕐 Apr–Oct 10–6. Guided tours Jul–Aug
🚌 From Thomastown
♿ Few
💷 Cheap

KILDARE ✪✪

This fine old county town has an attractive central square and some medieval buildings. St Brigid's Cathedral is on the site of a monastery founded in AD 490 and near by is a 10th-century round tower with wonderful views. The other tower in the town is that of the 15th-century castle.

Kildare is at the heart of horse-racing country, and Irish-bred horses are among the most prized in the world. The **National Stud** at Tully House gives visitors an insight into the development and control of these magnificent animals.

The **Japanese Gardens** at Tully House were landscaped in 1906 to 1910 by the Japanese gardener, Tasa Eida, and include a tea house and a miniature village carved from rock from Mount Fuji. The gardens symbolise the life of man, taking the pilgrim-soul on a journey from Birth to Eternity. Many rare plants are nurtured here, along with a collection of bonsai trees, and there is a lake, rich in the minerals which produce good bone formation in the horses – essential for potential winners.

✚ 31B3

National Stud/Japanese Gardens
✉ Tully House, Kildare
☎ 045-521617/ 522963
🕐 Mid-Feb–mid-Nov, daily 9:30–6.
🍴 Restaurant (££)
🚌 Bus from Kildare
♿ Few
💷 Expensive

> ### Did you know ?
>
> *Colonel William Hall-Walker, later Lord Wavertree, established the National Stud and the Japanese Gardens. He housed his racehorses in 'lantern' boxes with skylights so that the moon and stars could influence his thorough breeding programme. He would reject any foal born with an unfavourable astrological chart, and was surprisingly successful.*

KILKENNY (▶ 22, TOP TEN)

🚩 31C4

Malahide Castle
☎ 01-8462184/8462516
🕐 Apr–Oct:, Mon–Fri 10–5,
Sat 11–6, Sun & public
hols 11:30–6; Nov–Mar,
Mon–Fri 10–5, Sat, Sun &
public hols 2–5
🍴 Restaurant (££); coffee
shop (£)
🚌 42 from Dublin
💷 Moderate

🚩 31C5
✉ Near Drogheda
🕐 Always accessible
🍴 Buttergate Restaurant
(££), Millmount,
Drogheda

🚩 31C3
✉ Enniskerry
☎ 01-2046000
🕐 Mar–Oct, daily 9:30–5:30;
Nov–Feb 10:30–dusk
(waterfall open until 7 in
summer)
🍴 Tea room (£) kiosk at
waterfall
🚌 44 from Hawkins Street,
Dublin; 85 from DART
Bray station
♿ Good
💷 Moderate

MALAHIDE ⭐⭐

The town of Malahide is a traditional seaside resort that
has also become a popular residential area for commuters
to Dublin. One of its great attractions is that it is particularly
well endowed with good restaurants, but its main
attraction is the magnificent **castle**. It is one of Ireland's
oldest, with a romantic medieval outline that has changed
little in its 800 years, but the interior has been transformed
over the centuries, and now contains superb Irish furniture
and paintings, including a historic portrait collection which
is, in effect, a National Portrait Gallery.

MONASTERBOICE ⭐⭐

One of Ireland's best-known Christian sites,
Monasterboice was founded by St Buite in the 6th century
and thrived for 600 years, until the new Cistercian
Mellifont Abbey superceded it in importance. The site
includes a remarkable 10th-century round tower which
stands 33m high (without its roof) and offers a good view
of the encircling ramparts. There are also three superb high
crosses, of which the South Cross (Muiredach's) is the
best, a 6-m monolith with distinctive sculptural detail of
biblical scenes. The West Cross is the tallest, and has
some expressive carving, but has suffered from erosion.
The North Cross has a plain, modern shaft.

POWERSCOURT DEMESNE ⭐⭐⭐

Amidst the wild landscape of the Wicklow Mountains
(► 43) is one of the most superb gardens in Europe.
Powerscourt Gardens were originally laid out in the mid-
17th century to complement the magnificent Powerscourt
House, which tragically burned down in 1974, just after
extensive renovations. Great formal terraces step down
the south-facing slope, with distinctive mosaics of pebbles
(taken from the beach at Bray). There are beautiful lakes
and fountains, statues and decorative ironwork, American,

*The formal gardens at
Powerscourt are counted
among the finest in
Europe*

Italian and Japanese gardens and, in contrast, charming kitchen gardens and a little pet's cemetery. In every direction is a backdrop of mountain peaks.

Beyond the gardens, the deer park has a herd of sika deer, and Ireland's highest waterfall plunges 121m into a picturesque valley within the park.

The Glen of the Dargle is a wooded gorge, dotted with modern sculpture. A huge rock in the glen is known as Lover's Leap and has suitably melodramatic associations.

The loveliest 'power station' in Ireland, the Poulaphouca reservoir is part of the River Liffey hydroelectric scheme

THE WICKLOW MOUNTAINS ✪✪

Just a short distance from the centre of Dublin is this wonderfully secluded area of high mountains and peaceful valleys (▶ 45). Lugnaquilla is the highest point, at 943m, and is the source of the River Slaney. Two scenic passes cross the mountains from east to west – the Sally Gap 497m on the old Military Road and the Wicklow Gap further south, but be warned that the clouds can envelope these mountain tops, making driving very difficult.

Great forests clothe many of the mountain slopes, including Coollatin Park near Shillelagh, in the south, which preserves remnants of the oak forests which are said to have supplied the roof timbers for Dublin's St Patrick's Cathedral and London's Palace of Westminster. The Irish walking-stick-cum-weapon, the 'shillelagh', named after the village, were originally made of oak from the forests. Near Blessington is the great Poulaphouca Reservoir, providing Dublin with both water and electricity, with scenic lakeside drives and waterbus cruises.

Signs of habitation include ancient hillforts and stone circles, and the mountains offered the necessary tranquility for medieval monastic communities, such as Glendalough (▶ 40). Later still, the mansions of Powerscourt at Enniskerry and Russborough House, near Blessington took advantage of a wonderful mountain backdrop.

🔳 31C3
🍴 Poulaphouca House (£), Hollywood (☎ 045-864412)

✚ 31B1

Wexford Wildfowl Reserve
✚ 31C1
✉ North Slob
☎ 053-23129
🕐 Mid-Apr–Sep, daily 9–6;
Oct–mid-Apr, daily 10–5
🚌 No public transport to the
reserve
♿ Few; facilities being
improved
🎫 Free

*The attractive main street
in historic Wexford*

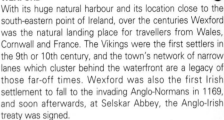

Irish Agricultural Museum
✉ Johnstown Castle, Old
Farmyard
☎ 053-42888
🕐 Jun–Aug, Mon–Fri 9–5,
Sat, Sun & bank hols 2–5;
Sep–May, Mon–Fri
1–12:30, 1:30–5, Sat, Sun
& bank hols 2–5. Closed
25 Dec–2 Jan, &
weekends mid-Nov–Mar
🍴 Coffee shop, Jul–Aug (£)
🚌 Westgate mini-tours from
Wexford Tourist Office
♿ Few 🎫 Moderate

44

WEXFORD ★

With its huge natural harbour and its location close to the south-eastern point of Ireland, over the centuries Wexford was the natural landing place for travellers from Wales, Cornwall and France. The Vikings were the first settlers in the 9th or 10th century, and the town's network of narrow lanes which cluster behind the waterfront are a legacy of those far-off times. Wexford was also the first Irish settlement to fall to the invading Anglo-Normans in 1169, and soon afterwards, at Selskar Abbey, the Anglo-Irish treaty was signed.

Wexford is an interesting mixture of working county town, with busy streets, lively pubs and a famous opera festival, and historic Heritage Town, with some of its 14th-century town wall still intact. After its award-winning restoration, the four-storey West Gate now houses the Heritage Centre, with an audio-visual presentation about the town.

The nearby mudflats known as The Slobs are now the **Wexford Wildfowl Reserve**, with a research station, a visitor centre, hides and a lookout tower. The reserve is of international importance, having one-third of the world's population of Greenland White-fronted geese.

About 6.5km south-west of the town is Johnstown Castle, home of the **Irish Agricultural Museum**, housed in historic estate farm buildings. It has a wide range of agricultural displays and replicas of a forge and other workshops.

Did you know ?

In the area of Bridgetown, to the south of Wexford, a distinct dialect exists. The people here use the oldest English speech in Ireland because the original Anglo–Norman colonists who arrived in the 12th century intermarried among themselves and were never assimilated by the native Irish.

A Tour of the Wicklow Mountains

This drive includes the beautiful Wicklow Mountains, two of Ireland's finest gardens and the monastic remains at Glendalough.

Leave Wicklow on the Dublin road and continue to Ashford.

Mount Usher Gardens, off to the right along the banks of the River Vartry, are a superb example of a 'wild gardens'.

In Ashford turn left, then fork right, following signs for 'Roundwood'. At the T-junction by Roundwood church, turn left, then fork right, signposted 'Enniskerry'. Continue, following signs for Enniskerry.

The entrance to the Powerscourt Demesne is on a bend at the beginning of the village. The gardens here are among the finest in Europe, and Powerscourt Waterfall is Ireland's Highest.

In Enniskerry, turn left, and after 8km reach Glencree. At the next junction head for 'Sally Gap, Glendalough'. After another 8km turn right, and keep following signs for 'Blessington' until reaching the N81. Turn left. After 3km turn left on to the R758 signposted 'Valleymount, Lake Drive'. Continue, following signs for Glendalough.

This ancient settlement is one of Ireland's major attractions, with atmospheric ruins.

Return to the junction and go forward through Laragh. After 5km turn right, signposted 'Arklow, Rathdrum R755'. In Rathdrum follow signs for 'Avoca'. At T-junction, turn left, then bear right, signposted 'Dublin'. After 13km turn right to return to Wicklow.

Distance
117km

Time
About 5–6 hours, depending on attractions visited

Start/end point
Wicklow
✠ 31C3

Lunch
Downshire House (££)
✉ Main Road, Blessington
☎ 045- 865199

Powerscourt waterfall, plunging 122m into the valley, is spectacular after heavy rain

The South

A great many visitors to Ireland head straight for this southwestern corner and ignore the rest of the country completely – which is a shame, but is entirely understandable. Here you will find the great fjord-like bays which cut into the rocky west coast, between the magnificent peninsulas of The Dingle, the Iveragh (better known as The Ring of Kerry), the Beara and the smaller, but no less beautiful Sheep's Head and Mizen peninsulas.

The south coast is less spectacular, but has some wonderful beaches, fine resorts and charming fishing villages such as Kinsale. Aim to be hungry when you visit here – the village is known as the Gourmet Capital of Ireland.

The southwest is not all coast and scenery. Ireland's second city, Cork, and its third, Limerick, are in this area, while towards the east are the historic city of Waterford, the great Rock of Cashel and the ancient towns and castles along the River Suir.

'Tis the bells of Shandon
That sound so grand on
The pleasant waters
of the River Lee.'

FATHER FRANCIS O'MAHONEY
(FATHER PROUT)
The Bells of Shandon (c1830s)

Cork

The Republic's second largest city, Cork is a busy commercial centre. At its heart is the wide St Patrick's Street, with lots of little lanes leading off which are a delight to explore. Cork has a unique character, standing firm against outside influences over the centuries and steadfastly refusing to play second fiddle to Dublin.

Cork is situated on an island in the River Lee, where it flows into the deep waters of Cork Harbour and it was the harbour that brought much of the city's prosperity over the years. It also brought the Vikings in AD 820, who burnt the settlement down, then rebuilt it as their own. Later the Anglo-Normans seized the city, but Cork was never inclined to give in easily to invading forces and suffered accordingly, notably at the hands of William of Orange in 1690 and during the 20th century, when it was again burned, this time by the notorious 'Black and Tans' as retribution for the city's stand against the British. As a result, this historic place, founded by St Finbarr in the 6th century, shows little signs of its longevity.

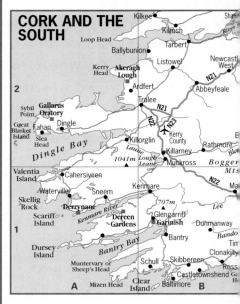

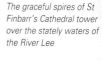

The graceful spires of St Finbarr's Cathedral tower over the stately waters of the River Lee

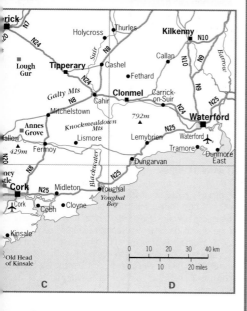

What to See in Cork

CORK CITY GAOL ✪✪

The thought of going to prison, if only for the afternoon, may not have an immediate appeal, but Cork's former gaol has been converted into a fascinating museum. The old cells have been furnished as they would have been during the 19th century, complete with lifelike figures and sound effects. There are exhibitions on the day-to-day life of prisoners and their guards.

CORK PUBLIC MUSEUM ✪

Few city museums have such a lovely setting as this. There are 7.5 hectares of beautiful parkland surrounding the Georgian House which now displays a wide range of collections illustrating the economic and social history of Cork, along with its Civic Regalia. Though the displays go back to prehistoric times, the main emphasis is on 19th- and 20th-century trades and crafts, including superb collections of silver, glass and needlepoint lace. The building was once the home of one of the Beamish family, whose brewery is still thriving in the city.

CRAWFORD ART GALLERY ✪✪

This superb art gallery, housed in a historic building, contains works of international and Irish interest, notably works by James Barry, Jack B Yeats and Sean Keating. Built in 1724 as the Custom House, it later became the home of the Royal Cork Institution, a scientific society. William Horatio Crawford, after whom the gallery is named, provided the funds for the gallery extension in 1884 and it also served as an art school for a time. The former school studios now house the modern galleries. Other rooms are dedicated to watercolours and prints, while the staircase carries a portrait collection and the top floor contains the Harry Clarke stained glass collection.

ST ANNE'S CHURCH ✪✪

The tall square tower of St Anne's, built in 1772 and capped by a gilded weather vane in the shape of a salmon, is Cork's best-known landmark. Its famous bells, which visitors can operate, chime each quarter hour. The interior of the church, no longer in use apart from one service on Sunday morning, is of warm wood, glowing in the light of its stained-glass windows. The composition *The Bells of Shandon* was written by Father Francis O'Mahoney, better known as 'Father Prout', a well-known literary figure of the 19th century.

49C1
⊠ Sunday's Well
☎ 021-305022
🕐 Mar–Oct, daily 9:30–5
🍴 Coffee shop (£)
🚌 From Grand Parade
♿ Good
✋ Moderate

49C1
⊠ Fitzgerald Park, Mardyke
☎ 021-270679
🕐 Mon–Fri 11–1, 2:15–5 (till 6, Jun–Aug), Sun 3–5. Closed Sat, bank hol weekends and public hols
🚌 8 from city centre
♿ None
✋ Free Mon–Fri

49C1
⊠ Emmet Place
☎ 021-273377
🕐 Mon–Sat 10–4:45. Closed 25 Dec–1 Jan, Sun and public hols
🍴 Crawford Gallery Restaurant (££)
🚌 All city buses
🚉 Cork (10-minute walk)
♿ Good
✋ Free

49C1
⊠ Church Street, Shandon
☎ 021-505906
🕐 Mon–Sat 10–4:30, Sun and bank hols by appointment
♿ None
✋ Moderate

A Walk Around Cork

The walk takes in the main shopping street and the art gallery, before crossing the River Lee to Shandon, then on to the Cork Public Museum in Fitzgerald Park.

Walk along Grand Parade away from the statue, then bear right into St Patrick Street. At the pedestrian crossing, turn left and go along Academy Street to the Crawford Art Gallery.

This fine municipal gallery has a particularly good collection of local landscapes.

Continue round the corner and cross the bridge. On the other side turn left, then bear right following signs to Shandon. At the Craft Centre turn right to reach St Anne's.

Now unused, this former church is one of Cork's great landmarks, with its lofty tower and famous bells.

Continue, passing the Shandon Arms on the left, and at the end go forward along Chapel Street.

Opposite the end of Chapel Street is the Cathedral of St Mary and St Ann, with a beautiful, bright interior and some interesting monuments.

Turn left along Cathedral Street, then left down Shandon Street to the river. Turn right to walk along the nearside riverbank, then at the end cross a footbridge. Follow the riverside wall then go forward between Mercy Hospital and Lee Maltings. At the end turn right and walk along Dyke Parade until you reach the gates to Fitzgerald Park on the right. The Cork Public Museum is just inside the gates.

Cork's city streets are an interesting mixture of wide boulevards and intriguing little alleyways

Distance
About 2.5km

Time
About 3 hours

Start point
Grand Parade
🚌 All city centre buses

End point
Fitzgerald Park
🚌 8 to city centre

Lunch
Oyster Tavern (£)
✉ Market Street
☎ 021-272716

What to See in The South

BANTRY

This lovely little town, at the head of the beautiful Bantry Bay, is a busy fishing port, its harbour overlooked by a statue of that intrepid Irish seafarer, St Brendan. Close by is the entrance to **Bantry House**, an exquisite Georgian mansion. The elegant interior contains a fine collection of furniture, Pompeiian mosaics and tapestries. The beautiful Italianate gardens have a wonderful view over the bay and delicate plants thrive in the mild climate.

THE BEARA PENINSULA

Less well known than the Ring of Kerry and The Dingle, The Beara Peninsula is just as beautiful, with its rocky, indented coastline and offshore islands. The Caha Mountains and the Slieve Miskish Mountains form its spine, creating a dramatic inland landscape and the Healy Pass, which zig-zags across the Caha range has wonderful views (▶ 59).

The **Sub-Tropical Gardens** on Garinish Island, in a sheltered inlet of Bantry Bay, reached by ferry from Glengarriff, is the Beara's main attraction. It is a magnificent Italian garden, with a world-famous collection of plants, which thrive here because of the warming effect of the Gulf Stream.

BLARNEY CASTLE

The 'gift of the Blarney' is known all over the world and this is where you get it. By leaning backwards over a sheer drop (protected by railings) from the castle battlements and kissing a particular piece of rock, any visitor can go home endowed with a new eloquence. The Blarney Stone is reached by ancient stone spiral staircases through the ruins of the 15th-century castle, which would be well worth a visit even without its notoriety. The castle is set in lovely grounds, and is one of Ireland's most visited places.

48B1

Bantry House
☎ 027-50047
🕐 Mid-Mar–Oct, daily 9–6
🍴 Coffee shop (£)
🚌 Cork–Bantry bus;
🚉 Cork
♿ Few 💰 Expensive

48A1

Sub-Tropical Gardens
✉ Garinish Island, off Glengarriff
☎ 027-63040
🕐 Mar, Oct, Mon–Sat 10–4:30, Sun 1–5; Apr–Jun & Sep, Mon–Sat 10–5:30, Sun 1–6; Jul & Aug, Mon– Sat 9:30–6, Sun 11–7 (last landing 1 hour before closing)
🚌 Glengarriff main street; Kenmare–Bantry bus passes through Glengarriff
🚉 Nearest railway station Killarney 59km
♿ Few
💰 Moderate (extra for ferry)

The gift of eloquence is not given away lightly at Blarney Castle

---

49C1
✉ Blarney, Co Cork
☎ 021-385252/385669
🕐 All year. Mon–Sat, May & Sep 9–6:30; Jun–Aug 9–7; Oct–Apr 9–6 or sunset; Sun 9:30–5:30 all year. Closed 24–25 Dec
♿ Few
💰 Moderate

CAHIR CASTLE ⭐

Dominating the market town of Cahir from a rock in the River Suir, Cahir Castle is one of the largest castles in Ireland. Built in the 15th century for the powerful Anglo-Norman Butler family, it is everyone's idea of the perfect medieval castle, with its thick curtain wall and great towers. It was besieged a number of times, most notably by the Earl of Essex in 1599, and cannonballs from this encounter are still embedded in the walls.

A 12th-century castle preceded the present one, and a Norman Festival is held each August.

✚ 49C2
✉ Cahir, Co Tipperary
☎ 052-41011
🕐 Apr–mid-Jun, mid-Sep–mid-Oct, daily 10–6; mid-Jun–mid-Sep, 9–7:30; mid-Oct–Mar, daily 10–1, 2–4:30
🚉 Railway station 0.5km
♿ Few
✋ Cheap

CASHEL ⭐⭐⭐

The town tends to be overshadowed by the great Rock of Cashel (▶ 25) which dominates the skyline, but as one of Ireland's Heritage Towns, it is well worth a visit in its own right. A good place to start is City Hall, which has historical and folklore displays relating to the town. There is also a Folk Village, with a series of 18th- to 20th-century house fronts, shops and memorabilia, and the Brù Borù Heritage Centre, which offers a cultural experience through its folk theatre, evening banquets, exhibitions and traditional music sessions.

✚ 49C2
🚌 Dublin–Cork buses
🚉 Thurles 18km
♿ Good

Folk Village
✉ Dominic Street
☎ 062-62525
🕐 Mar–May, daily 10–6; Jun–Sep, 9:30–7

Brù Borù Heritage Centre
☎ 062-61122
🕐 Mar–Jun daily 9:30–5:30; Jul–Aug daily 9:30–8; Sep–Feb Mon–Fri 9:30–5:30
🍽 Self-service restaurant (£). Combined evening meal and show (£££)
✋ Free; evening entertainment at Heritage Centre expensive

Beautiful Bantry Bay offers good fishing, and has a mussel farm too

53

DINGLE (➤ 19, TOP TEN)

THE RING OF KERRY ●●●

The road which encircles the Iveragh peninsula is popularly known as the Ring of Kerry, an exceptionally scenic circular route of 107km if you start and finish in Killarney. From here you go south through the National Park to Kenmare, then strike out along the north shore of the Kenmare estuary, through the lovely resort of Parknasilla. The famous Great Southern Hotel here has played host to the rich and famous for many years.

Farther along is Caherdaniel, where Daniel O'Connell was born. The route heads north from here around Ballinskelligs Bay to Waterville, then on to Cahersiveen, the 'capital' of the peninsula, with an interesting Heritage Centre. The road then heads eastwards, with Dingle Bay to the north, through Killorglin, a market town famous for its Puck Fair in August, then back to Killarney.

As if the wonderful coast and mountain scenery were not enough, the peninsula is also blessed with a warm Gulf Stream climate.

✚ 48A2
🛈 Killarny Tourist Information (☎ 064-31633)
🍴 Old Schoolhouse Restaurant (£), Knockeens, Cahersiveen (☎ 066-72426)

The nearest thing to commuters ever seen on the west Kerry coast

KILLARNEY ✪✪

Killarney is one of the busiest tourist towns in Ireland, not for its own attractions (though it has the **Transport Museum**) so much as for its surroundings. There are lots of interesting shops, pubs and restaurants here, but Killarney is essentially a base for exploring the beauties of Kerry, and is the traditional starting point for the Ring of Kerry. The Killarney National Park, 10,000 hectares of beautiful mountains, woodland and lakes, is right on the doorstep, and is the setting for **Muckross House** (► 23).

➕ 48B2

Transport Museum
✉ Scotts Hotel Gardens, East Avenue Road
☎ 064-32638
🕐 Mid-Mar–Oct, daily 10–6
♿ Free admission to wheelchair visitors
▣ Moderate

> ### *Did you know ?*
>
> *Jarveys are the drivers of the horse-drawn jaunting cars you will see lined up along the roadside in Killarney. Haggling over the fee is an acceptable part of the deal, but remember that you are not just paying to get from A to B – Jarveys are an intrinsic part of the Killarney experience and will usually spin a yarn or two along the way.*

KINSALE ✪✪✪

Kinsale is a delightful little harbour town and holiday resort, known as the 'Gourmet Capital of Ireland' because of its first-class restaurants, and for its Gourmet Festival which is held in October.

Historically, Kinsale is remembered for the 1601 battle, when a Spanish fleet came to aid Hugh O'Neill's struggle against the English. They captured the town and a siege ensued, but O'Neill's surprise attack was betrayed, part of the Irish army lost its way and the Spanish surrendered. As a result, many of the Irish aristocracy fled to Europe, leaving Ireland leaderless and defeated. Subsequently two massive fortresses were built to guard the harbour, and their ruins can still be seen.

It was off this coast that the *Lusitania* was sunk by a German submarine in 1915, with the loss of 1,500 lives, an event which drew the United States of America into World War I.

➕ 49C1
ℹ Tourist Information (☎ 021-772234)
🍴 Max's Wine Bar (££), Main Street (☎ 021-772443)

Imaginative paintwork on this Kinsale exterior reflects the village's close connection with both the sea and seafood

Food & Drink

Eating out in Ireland is as unhurried an experience as anything else in this relaxing island, and the generally high standard of cooking and service, and the quality of the ingredients, is certainly well worth savouring.

In all the major towns and cities there is a good variety of food on offer, and traditional Irish cuisine has enjoyed a revival, often with the occasional international influence.

Oysters and Guinness – food of the gods – are widely available around the coast from September to April

Away from the fast food places, eating out in Ireland is not particularly cheap, but travellers on a budget will find a choice of restaurants throughout the country which offer a 'tourist menu' of good food at reasonable prices.

Specialities to look out for include local cheeses, of which there are many, such as the delicious Cashel Blue, Cooleeney, St Killian, Durrus, Chetwynd Blue and Mizen. Irish seafood is also legendary, with fresh lobster, oysters, mussels and scallops.

Irish Cuisine

Irish cooking has a reputation for being plain, but plentiful, which does it something of a disservice, because the traditional dishes have wonderfully rich flavours and interesting taste combinations.

In recent years dishes that were designed to satisfy the hunger of hard-working farmers and fishermen have been adapted to suit the lesser appetites of those who have done no more than a bit of gentle sightseeing. What was once dismissed as 'peasant food' has now become a delicacy, such as *drisheen* (black pudding), *cruibeens* (pigs' trotters), Dublin coddle (a sausage stew), beef stewed in Guinness and, of course, Irish stew. Potato dishes such as Champ (mashed with chives and butter) or Colcannon (mashed, mixed with leek, butter, cabbage, cream and nutmeg) are a tasty accompaniment, and adventurous diners can sample edible seaweed in the form of dulce or carrageen pudding.

Irish bread is not just something to make a sandwich with. There are lots of tasty varieties that only need a

'Bog Butter'
In the days long before refrigerators, butter was stored in wooden barrels, buried in the peat bogs. Not only did it stay fresh for a long time, it was safe from butter burglars. 'Bog Butter' is still unearthed occasionally during peat cutting.

spreading of butter or a side dish of home-made soup. Soda bread, or wheaten bread, made with stone-ground flour, has a wonderful flavour and texture and there are lots of fruity tea breads such as Barm brack. There is even a potato bread (mashed potato mixed with flour and egg) that is cooked on a griddle and often served with the enormous traditional Irish breakfast of bacon, eggs, sausage and black (or white) pudding.

Whiskey and Beer

Think of Irish beer and it is probably a pint of Guinness that springs to mind. Sold in at least 30 countries world-wide, Guinness is a great symbol of Irishness, but undoubtedly tastes best on Irish soil, with its cool, biting taste and thick creamy head. Hard on the heels of Guinness are two other stouts, Beamish and Murphy's, both brewed in Cork, while Smithwicks offer a smooth-tasting bitter which is similar to English beer. Lager is also widely available to those who prefer a more continental taste.

Irish whiskey also has a world market and has a wonderful clean flavour, quite different from Scotch whisky or American bourbon. Four main brands are produced by the Irish Distillers company – Bushmills, Jameson, Powers and Paddy, with pure malts of various ages as well as blended whiskey. The Bushmills Distillery in Northern Ireland and Jameson's at Midleton, Co Cork give guided tours which explain the distilling process.

Breweries and Distilleries
At one time Cork had 10 distilleries and 30 breweries. Now there are just two breweries – Beamish and Murphy's – and an Irish Distillers' plant. This company, a subsidiary of the French Ricard (Pernod) company, actually produces all of the Irish whiskey brands. Just east of the city, at Midleton, the Jameson Heritage Centre tells the history of Irish whiskey.

WHAT TO SEE

+ 48C2

Hunt Museum

✉ University of Limerick
☎ 061-312833/33644
🕐 Mon–Sat 10–5
🍴 Restaurant (£)
♿ Very good
✋ Moderate

King John's Castle

✚ Nicholas Street, King's Island
☎ 061-411201/361511
🕐 Apr–Oct, daily 9:30–5:30; Nov–Apr, Sun 11–4:30 (last admission 1 hour before closing)
🍴 Coffee shop (£)
♿ Very good
✋ Moderate

LIMERICK ✪✪

The Republic's third largest city, Limerick is an attractive, prosperous and lively place with a long and distinguished history. It is also a cultural centre, well endowed with art galleries, museums – notably the **Hunt Museum** at the university, which has a superb collection of Celtic to medieval treasures – and theatres, and hosts a number of festivals and events throughout the year.

The wide River Shannon flows through the city, overlooked by the massive **King John's Castle** and crossed by many fine bridges. The oldest part of the city is on King's Island, first settled by the Vikings, and it is here that the most important historical sites are found, including the castle and the 12th-century Protestant cathedral.

There is fine architecture to be seen all around the city, jealously guarded by the Limerick Civic Trust. The best old street is The Crescent, while modern architecture is superbly demonstrated in the Civic Centre and City Hall on Merchant's Quay.

Did you know ?

The first Waterford Glass factory was opened by George and William Penrose in 1783 and some of their work can be seen in Waterford City Hall, but the factory soon closed down, only to reopen in 1947. There is a gallery, and tours of the factory include the furnaces, glass blowing, annealing and cutting.

+ 49D2

Waterford Crystal Visitor Centre

✉ N25 Cork road
☎ 051-73311
🕐 Apr–Oct, daily 8:30–4 (shop open till 6); Nov–Mar: Mon–Thu 9–3:15 (shop open Mon–Fri till 5)
🍴 Restaurant (£)
🚌 Waterford–Ballybeg
♿ Good ✋ Moderate

WATERFORD ✪✪

Waterford grew from an ancient Viking settlement into the foremost port in Ireland, and its quays are still busy with international trade; the famous **Waterford Crystal Visitor Centre** reflects this. The city preserves an atmosphere of the past, and the mixture of Celt, Viking, Norman, English, Flemish and Huguenot gives a European flavour which is reflected on the sea front and in its narrow lanes. One of the oldest buildings is Reginald's Tower, built by the Vikings in 1003, which now houses the city museum. The Church of Ireland cathedral is regarded as the finest 18th-century ecclesiastical building in Ireland, and the Catholic cathedral has a wonderful interior, with superb carving and stained glass.

Spectacular Scenery in Kerry & Cork

This drive includes the wonderful wooded mountains of the Killarney National Park, the spectacular Healy Pass and two of Ireland's finest historic houses.

From Killarney take the N71, signposted 'Muckross', and soon reach the Killarney National Park and Muckross House.

Muckross is one of Ireland's leading stately homes, and its situation amidst the mountains and lakes of the national park is unsurpassed.

Continue on the N71, passing Torc Waterfall, to reach Ladies View, then after 6km, at Molls Gap, bear left, signposted 'Kenmare, Glengarriff'. At Kenmare drive up the main street and turn right, then leave the town following signs for Glengarriff and Bantry. Cross a river bridge and turn right, signposted 'Castletown Bearhaven R571'. Continue for about 14km then follow signs for Healy Pass.

This pass across the Caha Mountains has stunning views and a breathtaking summit.

Over the top of the pass, descend a series of hairpin bends and continue to reach a T-junction. Turn left for Glengarriff.

Garinish Island, with its beautiful sub-tropical gardens, can be reached by ferry from Glengarriff.

Continue for 5.6km to Bantry.

By the harbour on the Cork road is Bantry House and the Armada Exhibition.

Retrace the route to Glengarriff, then take the N71 to Kenmare and Killarney.

Distance
140km

Time
6–7 hours depending on attractions visited

Start/end point
Killarney
48B2

Lunch
D'Arcy's (££)
Main Street, Kenmare
064-41589
Closed Mon

Ladies View is a spectacular viewpoint high above the Killarney National Park

The West

The wild beauty of the west is underlaid with the hostility of a landscape that does its best to defy cultivation. There are fields, but they are the size of pocket handkerchiefs, and the drystone walls that enclose them have by no means used up all of the land's loose rocks.

Vast empty areas of blanket bog have pockets of wetness, which expand into a network of lakes and rivers beneath the mountains of Connemara and Joyce's Country. The great Loughs – Conn, Mask and Corrib – lie between Sligo and Galway Bays. Further east the River Shannon forms the backbone of a watery highway.

In Clare, The Burren is a moonscape of bare limestone, where plants cling onto the sparse soil, and the western boundary of all this is a jagged and spectacular coastline.

The main towns – Galway, Sligo, Westport, Ballina and Ennis – are lively and attractive while elsewhere there are tiny villages.

'I hear lake water
lapping with low
sounds by the shore…
I hear it in the deep
heart's core.'

W B YEATS
The Lake Isle of Innisfree
(1893)

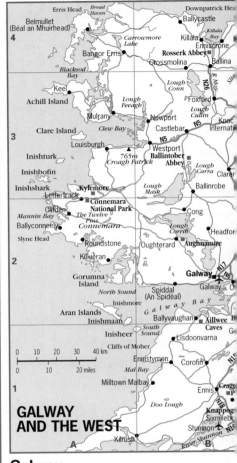

GALWAY AND THE WEST

Map labels:

Erris Head, Broad Haven, Downpatrick Hea
Belmullet (Béal an Mhuirhead), Ballycastle
Carrowmore Lake, Killala, Killala Bay, Enniscrone
Bangor Erris, Rosserk Abbey, Crossmolina, Ballina
Blacksod Bay, Lough Conn, N26, Foxford, R. Mo, Slig
Keel, Lough Feeagh, Lough Cullin, Knoc
Achill Island, Mulrany, Newport, Castlebar, Internati
Clare Island, Clew Bay, N5
Louisburgh, Westport, N5
765m Croagh Patrick, Ballintober Abbey, Lough Carra, Clarer
Inishturk, Lough Mask, Ballinrobe
Inishbofin
Inishshark, Letterfrack, Kylemore, Connemara National Park, Cong
Clifden, The Twelve Pins, Lough Corrib, Headfor
Mannin Bay, Connemara
Ballyconneely, Slyne Head, Roundstone, Oughterard, Aughnanure
Kilkieran, Galway, M17, N6
Gorumna Island, Galway
North Sound, Spiddal (An Spidéal), Galway Bay
Inishmore, South Sound, Ballyvaughan, Aillwee Caves, G
Aran Islands, Inishmaan, Lisdoonvarna
Inisheer, Cliffs of Moher
Ennistymon, Corofin, N1
Mal Bay
Milltown Malbay, Ennis, Cragg, P
Doo Lough, Knappog, Sixmileb
Kilrush, Shannon, River Shannon, N1

0 10 20 30 40 km
0 10 20 miles

Galway

Galway, the historic capital of Connaught, is Ireland's fourth largest city, with a delightful blend of ancient and modern. Though it is surrounded by the urban sprawl of industry and superstores, it has at its heart a maze of narrow streets, lined with a mixture of modern shop fronts, traditional-style painted façades, old pubs and restaurants. A relaxed west coast atmosphere prevails, tempered by a lively student population.

Situated in the northeast corner of Galway Bay, where the River Corrib pours into the sea, Galway was built on international trade and sea fishing, and its oldest parts cluster

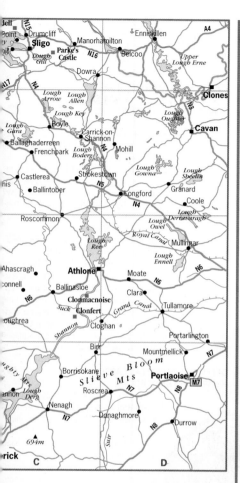

The harbour at Kilkieran is typical of Ireland's little fishing communities

around the harbour and riverside quays. On the east bank is the Spanish Arch, the city's most famous landmark, built to protect cargoes of wine and brandy from Iberia.

Behind the quay is a network of narrow streets, leading off from an equally narrow main thoroughfare. A modern-shopping mall, incorporating part of the medieval city wall, is hidden away behind old façades.

On the far side of the river is The Claddagh, once a close-knit Gaelic-speaking fishing community and now remembered in the continuing tradition of the Claddagh ring, with two hands holding a crowned heart.

Galway is a lively centre for the arts, with many events, concerts and festivals throughout the year. The most famous is the International Oyster Festival in September.

What to See in Galway

 62B2
✉ Bowling Green
☎ 091-567641
🕐 Mar–Oct, daily 10–5:15;
Nov–Feb, daily 2–4
✋ Cheap

NORA BARNACLE HOUSE MUSEUM ✪

Built around the turn of the century, this tiny cottage, in a quiet street close to the city centre, is now the smallest museum in Ireland. It was the home of Nora Barnacle, companion, wife and lifelong inspiration of James Joyce, and even without all the memorabilia, it is impossible to ignore the romantic associations. It was here, in 1909, that Joyce first met Nora's mother, and the house now contains letters, photographs and other exhibits on the lives of the couple.

✚ 62B2
✉ The Quay
☎ 091-567641
🕐 Mar–Oct, daily 10–5:15;
Nov–Feb, daily 2–4
♿ None
✋ Cheap

SPANISH ARCH CIVIC MUSEUM ✪✪✪

Galway's city walls were built between the 13th and 17th centuries, and the Spanish Arch dates from 1584, when the walls were extended. Its purpose was to protect cargoes of wine and brandy as they were being unloaded on the quay. Adjoining the arch, Galway City Museum contains a range of displays which relate the long and eventful history of the city, including a large map of Galway in 1651 and photographs and artefacts of the Claddagh settlement before its old cottages were dismantled.

✚ 62B2
ℹ Tourist Information
(☎ 091-563081)
🍴 GBC Restaurant and
Coffee Shop (£),
7 Williamsgate
Street

CATHEDRAL OF OUR LADY ASSUMED INTO ✪
HEAVEN AND ST NICHOLAS

Overlooking the River Corrib near the Salmon Weir Bridge, this splendid modern Roman Catholic cathedral opened in 1965 and looked so grand that the locals dubbed it the 'Taj Michael', after the then Bishop of Galway, Michael (pronounced Mee-hawl) Brown.

Built on the site of the former county gaol, the neo-Renaissance building is topped by a great copper dome, and the interior is plain but impressive, with floors of Connemara marble, rough-hewn limestone walls and superb stained glass. It was designed by John J Robinson and replaced the former cathedral on the corner of Abbeygate Street, which has been converted into shops.

Christopher Columbus is said to have prayed in Galway's church of St Nicholas

A Walk Around Galway

From Eyre Square, the heart of the city, walk along William Street, Shop Street and High Street. Reach a cobbled crossroads and keep forward along Quay Street.

On the corner is Claddagh Gold, a little jeweller's shop with a Claddagh Ring Museum in the back room. At the end is the famous Spanish Arch, where Iberian traders would land their cargoes, and the adjacent Galway City Museum.

Take the riverside path that leads off between the bridge and Jury's Hotel. Cross the next road and continue alongside the river on your left, and a canal on your right. At the end of the path, cross a footbridge over the canal, then turn left and walk to the Salmon Weir Bridge. Cross the bridge and the Cathedral of Our Lady Assumed into Heaven and St Nicholas is immediately ahead.

The Cathedral, completed in 1965, is topped by a great copper dome. The interior is light, spacious and, though plain, is very impressive.

Recross the bridge and turn right down Newtown Smith, passing the footbridge crossed earlier. Keep forward, turn right at the crossroads, then at the end bear left. About halfway along on the right is Nora Barnacle's House.

This tiny cottage is where the writer James Joyce courted his future wife. Mementoes of the couple are on display.

At the end, opposite St Nicholas Church, turn left into Market Street, then right into Upper Abbeygate Street.

The building at the end, on the right, is Lynch's Castle, now occupied by the Allied Irish Bank.

Turn left into William Street and return to Eyre Square.

Distance
About 2km

Time
2–3 hours

Start/end point
Eyre Square
🚌 All city centre buses

Lunch
Hooker Jimmy's (££)
✉ The Fishmarket, Spanish Arch
☎ 091-568351

What to See in The West

ARAN ISLANDS (► 16, TOP TEN)

BUNRATTY CASTLE AND FOLK PARK ✪✪✪

Bunratty, 14.5km northeast of Limerick, is Ireland's most complete medieval castle, thanks to the superb restoration work done in 1960 when the former ruin was purchased by Bord Failte and Lord Gort. Following the restoration, Lord Gort installed his collections of furniture, *objets d'art*, paintings and tapestries, all of which predate 1650. The castle has become famous for its medieval banquets, with historic costume and traditional food and entertainment.

In the castle grounds, Irish village life at the turn of the century has been re-created, with reconstructed urban and rural dwellings, farmhouses, a watermill, forge and village street, complete with shops and a pub.

THE BURREN AND AILLWEE CAVE ✪✪✪

The Burren National Park preserves a remarkable landscape which continues to excite geologists and botanists from far and wide. It is a vast plateau of limestone hills which were scraped free of their soil by retreating glaciers 15,000 years ago, then eroded by rain and Atlantic mists. The tiny amounts of soil which gather in the rock fissures support both Alpine and Mediterranean plant life, and early summer is the main flowering season.

🕀 62B1
✉ N18 Bunratty
☎ 061-361511/360788
🕐 Sep–Jun, daily 9:30–4:15
🍽 Tea room (£); lunches in barn May–Oct (£); Mac's Pub (££)
🚌 From Limerick, Ennis and Shannon
🚉 Limerick and Ennis
♿ Few
💷 Expensive

🕀 62B2
Aillwee Cave
✉ Ballyvaughan
☎ 065-77036
🕐 Mid-Mar–Nov, 10–5:30 (6:30 Jul–Aug)
🍽 Coffee shop, fast food (£)
🚌 From Galway
♿ Few   💷 Expensive

The Burren Display Centre in the village of Kilfenora illustrates the complexity of the geology, flora, fauna and settlements of the area. Caves are another feature of the limestone karst; a prime example is **Aillwee Cave**, south of Ballyvaughan, which has fossil formations and water figures. The Burren is best appreciated on foot, and the waymarked 42-km Burren Way, running from Ballyvaughan and Liscannor, can be undertaken in short sections.

Did you know ?

Lisdoonvarna, at the heart of the Burren, is the only active spa resort in Ireland, with Sulphur and Chalybeate springs. The town is also famous for its Matchmaking Festival in September, traditionally held after the harvest so that farmers can spare the time to seek a partner.

CLIFFS OF MOHER ✪✪✪

These towering cliffs rise sheer out of the turbulent Atlantic to a height of nearly 213m and stretch for 8km along the Clare coast north of Hag's Head. Majestic in calm weather, the cliffs are most dramatic (and dangerous) when stormy seas crash into their base, hurling pebbles high up into the air. Horizontal layers of flagstones have been exposed by coastal erosion, making convenient perches for the sea birds, including puffins, which abound here. At the highest point of the cliffs, O'Brien's Tower was constructed in the early 19th century as a lookout point for the first tourists, and gives views of the Clare Coastline, the Aran Islands and mountains as far apart as Kerry and Connemara. It now includes a visitor centre.

CLONMACNOISE (▶ 18, TOP TEN)

🔲 62B1

O'Brien's Tower and Visitor Centre
⊠ Near Liscannor
☎ 065-81565/360788
🕐 Mar–Oct, daily 10–6 (subject to weather conditions)
🍴 Tea room (£)
🚌 From Lahinch and other nearby towns
♿ First viewing platform accessible to wheelchairs, but not tower
✋ Cheap

Two geological marvels of County Clare: the Burren, opposite, and the towering Cliffs of Moher

➕ 62A2

National Park Visitor Centre
✉ Letterfrack
☎ 095-41054/41006
🕐 Apr–mid-Oct, 9:30–6:30;
   Mid-Oct–Mar, 10–5
🍴 Tea rooms (£)
♿ Good
💰 Cheap
❓ Guided walks Jul–Aug;
   programme of talks

CONNEMARA ✪✪✪

To the northwest of Galway City is Connemara, which has some of the most dramatic scenery in Ireland. Much of its convoluted coastline, with masses of tiny islands and some excellent beaches, can be followed by road – narrow and bumpy for the most part, so do not expect to get anywhere fast – and the views are spectacular. Inland, in southern Connemara, are thousands of lakes amidst the bogland. Further north, and hardly ever out of sight, are the brooding ranges of the Twelve Pins and the Maumturk Mountains. Connemara Marble is quarried at Recess, and there is a factory shop and showroom at Connemara Marble Industries in Moycullen (► 106).

A landscape laced with glittering lakes near Screeb, Connemara

The Connemara National Park protects about 2,000 hectares of the mountains, bogs, heaths and grasslands, and there is a good visitor centre in Letterfrack, with exhibitions, audio-visuals, nature trails, information – and a herd of Connemara ponies.

➕ 62B1
✉ Near Quin
☎ 061-360788
🕐 Apr–Oct 9:30–4:40
🍴 Refreshments (£)
♿ Good
💰 Moderate

KNAPPOGUE CASTLE ✪✪

Built in the mid-15th century for the MacNamaras, Knappogue underwent many changes over the course of the next five centuries. It was extended and adapted and used as government offices for a while, before falling into a ruinous state. In the 1960s it was acquired by Mark Edwin Andrews, then Assistant Secretary to the US Navy. He and his wife set about the task of restructuring the castle into an authentic setting for the medieval banquets which continue to be popular. They include dinner and a pageant, with stories of the history of the women of Ireland – real and legendary. The castle was acquired by the Shannon Development Company in 1996.

LISSADELL HOUSE ⭐

Lissadell House has been the home of the illustrious Gore-Booth family since it was built in the 19th century. A late Georgian mansion, it was the home of Sir Henry Gore-Booth (1843–1900), the Arctic explorer. One frequent visitor was William Butler Yeats, who was a friend of Henry's daughters, Eva, also a poet, and Constance, later Countess Markievicz, the most notorious member of the family. She was a passionate member of Sinn Féin and was the only aristocrat in the Citizen Army, fighting for the liberation of Ireland. Heroine of the 1916 uprising, she was sentenced to death, but the sentence was commuted and she was released in 1917. Countess Markievicz went on to become the first woman elected to the House of Commons (but refused to take her seat at Westminster) and was Minister for Labour in the first Irish government.

THE SHANNON ⭐⭐

Ireland's longest river, the Shannon rises in a humble pool (called the Shannon Pot) in County Cavan, then gathers strength as it flows through a series of lakes before it meets the Atlantic beyond Limerick. Historically, river crossings were always strategic points, where towns grew and prospered – places such as Athlone and Carrick-on-Shannon, which are both bases for the leisure cruiser holidays for which this mighty river is so popular. Anglers, too, find this river one of the most rewarding in Europe for its variety of fish.

🚩 63C4
✉ Carney
☎ 071-63150
🕐 Jun–mid-Sep, Mon–Sat 10:30–12:15, 2–4:30. Closed Sun
🚌 From Sligo
♿ Good
🎫 Moderate

🚩 62B1
🚢 Shannon–Erne Waterway Ltd (☎ 078 44855)

Great literary gatherings took place within the walls of Lissadell House

69

Westport House is one of the greatest attractions in northwest Ireland

➕ 63C4
ℹ️ Tourist Information
 (☎ 071-61201)
🍴 Embassy Restaurant (££)

SLIGO ✪✪

Sligo is a lively and attractive town with splendid old shop-fronts and traditional music pubs. It is also a significant cultural centre and has a fine range of art galleries and museums, as well as the various festivals which take place throughout the year.

Over 1,000 years of history have shaped the town, but it is literature that attracts many of its visitors. This is Yeats country, and the subject of one of his best known poems is just outside the town – the Isle of Inisfree in Lough Gill (riverboat trips to the lough depart from Sligo's Doorly Park). Sligo has many other attractions including its two fine cathedrals and Sligo Abbey, a Dominican friary founded in 1252.

➕ 62B2
✉️ Gort
☎ 091-631436
🕐 Easter–Sep, daily 10–6
🍴 Refreshments (£)
♿ Few
👆 Moderate
❓ Audio-visual presentation and displays of first editions

THOOR BALLYLEE ✪✪

In 1917 the poet William Butler Yeats bought the derelict 16th-century tower house and renovated it. For the next 12 years he and his family spent their summers here and it was in these peaceful surroundings that he wrote most of his works. His friend and patron, Lady Gregory, lived near by, and together they were the inspiration behind the Irish Literary Revival and the founding of the Abbey Theatre in Dublin. In the 1960s Thoor Ballylee was again restored, to show how it looked when Yeats was here, and, when completed, was opened to the public.

➕ 62B3

Westport House
✉️ The Quay, Westport
☎ 098-25430
🕐 Late Mar–late Jun daily 2–6; late Jun–late Aug, Mon–Fri 10:30–6, Sun 2–6
🍴 Refreshments (£)
♿ Few
👆 Expensive

WESTPORT ✪✪

Set on Clew Bay, Westport is one of the liveliest and most charming towns in the west of Ireland, with broad Georgian streets and a leafy riverside avenue at its heart. Nearby **Westport House** dates from the 1730s and has wholeheartedly embraced its role as the only stately home open to the public in Sligo. It is beautifully furnished and has some superb Waterford crystal, silver and paintings. The dungeons are from an earlier building, reputedly a castle of Grace O'Malley, the 16th-century pirate queen.

The grounds include a zoo, model railway, boating lake and horse-drawn caravans.

The Coast, Lakes & Mountains of Connemara

This drive follows the coastline for much of the way, with views of the Aran Islands in the early stages. It then passes through isolated settlements amidst a rocky landscape, with mountain views, to end at the lovely little town of Clifden.

From Galway follow signs for Salthill until a roundabout on the seafront, then take the Spiddal road west along Galway Bay. At the T-junction turn left, signposted Carraroe and Barna, then after about 13km pass through Spiddal.

There are breathtaking views along the coast and across Galway Bay before the road swings right to open up an inland vista of distant mountains.

Turn right on to the R336, signed 'Cill Ciarain, Scriob, Carna and Ros Muc', then after 11.2km at a T-junction, make a left turn signed 'Connemara Scenic Route'. Continue through Cill Ciarain (Kilkieran), then after 8.4km bear right, signed 'Clifden', with views of the Twelve Pins ahead. Turn left on to the R342 and follow signs for Roundstone.

This charming village is the home of Malachy Kearns' *bodhrán* workshop, where the craftsmen can often be seen making his traditional Irish drums. There is also a pottery close by.

After 13.2km reach Ballyconneely and continue around the rocky bay, then turn left into Clifden after a further 9.2km.

If you want to complete the circle, the road back to Galway (about 48km) is straightforward and well signposted, passing through magnificent scenery.

Distance
112km

Time
About 5 hours, including stop for lunch and visits to craft workshops

Start point
Galway
✚ 62B2

End point
Clifden
✚ 62A2

Lunch
Cashel House Hotel (£££)
✉ Cashel
☎ 095-31001

A romantic neo-Gothic mansion in a wonderful setting, Kylemore Abbey is now a girls' convent school

The North

When Brendan Behan said 'there is no such thing as bad publicity'... he could not have contemplated the task of promoting the six counties of Northern Ireland (sometimes referred to as Ulster) as a tourist destination. The unfortunate reputation engendered by the Province's notorious trouble spots deters many, and this is a great shame because they are missing some of the most beautiful scenery in Europe.

The coast of Antrim offers a spectacular drive past the lovely Glens of Antrim before the route swings around to the west to reach the Giant's Causeway. Further south the Mountains of Mourne sweep down to the sea. Inland are forest parks, lakes and mountains, historic towns, ancient sites and, of course, Belfast, a busy city with an industrial heritage and a lively arts scene. This section also includes the far northwestern part of the Republic, Co Donegal, famous for its beaches and tweed.

'England and Ireland may flourish together. The world is large enough for us both. Let it be our care not to make ourselves too little for it.'

EDMUND BURKE
Letter to Samuel Span, Esq (1778)

Belfast

The capital of Northern Ireland is a relatively young city, which grew rapidly in Victorian times, when its linen and shipbuilding industries flourished and the city doubled in size every 10 years. Today it has a quite unique character, brought about by the culmination of hard work, hard times and a particular brand of Irish humour. The redevelopment of its dockyard areas is giving a welcome facelift to the eastern flank of the city centre.

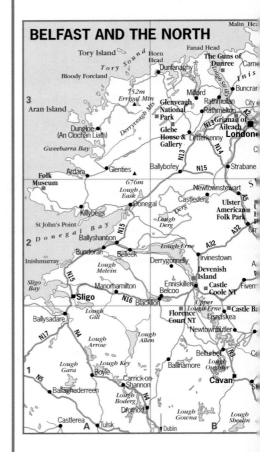

BELFAST AND THE NORTH

Malin He

Tory Island

Tory Sound

Horn Head

Fanad Head

The Guns of Dunree Carn

Dunfanaghy

nis

Bloody Foreland

752m
Errigal Mtn

Miltord

Rathmullan
City

3

Aran Island

Glenveagh
National
Park

Rathmelton

N13 Grianan of
Aileach London

Dungloe
(An Clochan Liath)

Glebe
House &
Gallery

Letterkenny

N14

C

Gweebarra Bay

Ballybofey

N15

Strabane

Folk
Museum

Ardara

Glenties

676m
Lough
Eask

Newtownstewart

Castlederg

Ulster
American
Folk Park

Killybegs

Donegal

Lough
Derg

St John's Point

Ballyshannon

Lough Erne

A32

2

D o n e g a l   B a y

Bundoran

Belleek

Derrygonnelly

Irvinestown

Inishmurray

Lough
Melvin

Devenish
Island

Sligo
Bay

Manorhamilton

Enniskillen
Belcoo

Castle
Coole NT

Fiven

Sligo

N16 Blacklion

Upper
Lough Erne Castle B

Florence
Court NT

Lisnaskea

Ballysadare

Lough
Gill

Newtownbutler

N17

Lough
Arrow

N4

Lough
Allen

Belturbet

Lough
Gara

Lough
Key

Ballinamore

Lough
Oughter

N5

Ballaghaderreen

Boyle

Carrick-on-
Shannon

Cavan

Lough
Bodery

N4

Dromod

Lough
Gowna

Lough
Sheelin

Castlerea

Tulsk

Dublin

A

B

Belfast's industrial past, together with the disturbing images of the recent troubles, can conjure up a somewhat misleading picture for those who have never visited the city. Its Victorian prosperity has left a legacy of magnificent public buildings and monuments, finance houses and warehouses.

At the heart of the city is the spacious and leafy Donegall Square, dominated by the magnificent City Hall, and surrounded by the main shopping streets.

Belfast has superb museums, libraries and art galleries, excellent shopping and a lively and varied cultural life, from grand opera to informal traditional music sessions.

Beautiful parks and gardens include the famous Botanic Gardens and the canal-side Lagan Valley Regional Park, but the most spectacular is on the slopes of Cave Hill to the north, which incorporates the zoo, Belfast Castle and a heritage centre.

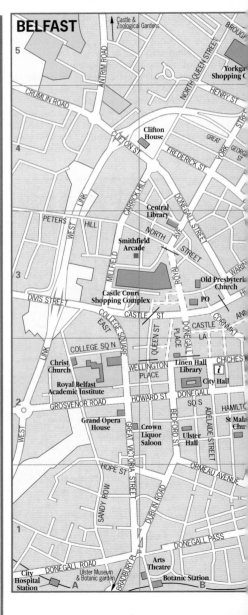

BELFAST

↑ Castle & Zoological Gardens

5

ANTRIM ROAD

NORTH QUEEN STREET

BROUGH

Yorkga Shopping C

CRUMLIN ROAD

HENRY ST

Clifton House

CLIFTON ST

GREAT

YORK

GEORGE

STREET

4

FREDERICK ST

LINK

WEST

CARRICK HILL

Central Library

DONEGALL STREET

PETERS

HILL

NORTH

STREET

3

MILLFIELD

Smithfield Arcade

ROYAL

WARIN

Old Presbyteria Church

DIVIS STREET

Castle Court Shopping Complex

CASTLE ST

PO

HI

COLLEGE SQUARE EAST

DONEGALL PLACE

CORNMKT

ANN

CASTLE

LA

COLLEGE SQ N

Christ Church

Royal Belfast Academic Institute

QUEEN ST

WELLINGTON PLACE

Linen Hall Library

CHICHES

i

City Hall

2

GROSVENOR ROAD

HOWARD ST

DONEGALL SQ S

HAMILTO

WEST LINK

Grand Opera House

GREAT VICTORIA STREET

Crown Liquor Saloon

BEDFORD ST

Ulster Hall

ADELAIDE STREET

St Mala Chur

HOPE ST

ORMEAU AVENUE

SANDY ROW

DUBLIN ROAD

1

DONEGALL PASS

DONEGALL ROAD

City Hospital Station

Ulster Museum & Botanic garden

BRADBURY PL

Arts Theatre

Botanic Station

A

B

A detail of the ornate exterior of Belfast's Grand Opera House

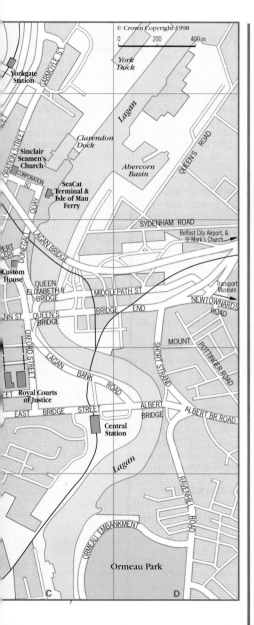

© Crown Copyright 1998

0   200   400 m

York
Dock

Lagan

Yorkgate
Station

CARMOYLE ST.

CORPORATION STREET

*Clarendon
Dock*

QUEEN'S ROAD

Sinclair
Seamen's
Church

CORPORATION
SQ

*Abercorn
Basin*

SeaCat
Terminal &
Isle of Man
Ferry

SYDENHAM ROAD

DONEGALL QUAY

Belfast City Airport, &
St Mark's Church

ERT
ARE

LAGAN BRIDGE

Custom
House

QUEEN
ELIZABETH II
BRIDGE

MIDDLEPATH ST.

Transport
Museum

NEWTOWNARDS
ROAD

NN ST.

QUEEN'S
BRIDGE

BRIDGE   END

OXFORD STREET

MOUNT

POTTINGER ROAD

LAGAN   BANK   ROAD

SHORT STRAND

Royal Courts
of Justice

EAST   BRIDGE   STREET

ALBERT
BRIDGE

ALBERT BR ROAD

Central
Station

Lagan

RAVENHILL ROAD

ORMEAU EMBANKMENT

Ormeau Park

C   D

*The splendid Victorian
palm house at Belfast
Botanic Gardens*

What to See in Belfast

CITY HALL ✪✪

In 1906 Belfast's sumptuously decorated City Hall was completed, a celebration in stone of the granting of city status by Queen Victoria. Its two storeys are set around a central courtyard and the building is topped by a tall copper dome which rises above the central staircase at the heart of an exuberant interior of rich mosaic, stained glass, marble and wood panelling. The grounds are dotted with fine statues and monuments including, inevitably, one of Queen Victoria.

BOTANIC GARDEN ✪✪

The Botanic Garden is a wonderful place to wander away from the bustle of the city. It includes a fragrant rose garden, formal beds and herbaceous borders, and among the outstanding greenhouses is the Palm House. Begun in 1838, it is a remarkable cast-iron curvilinear structure in which tropical flowering plants thrive. There is also a Tropical Ravine, a deep glen with a high level walkway from which visitors can look down over some enormous tropical plants.

CROWN LIQUOR SALOON ✪✪✪

High Victorian décor is preserved in this pub, which has been restored and is now in the care of the National Trust. It is no museum piece, though – the Crown is managed by a brewery and is open for business as usual. The tiled exterior, with Corinthian pillars flanking the doorway, gives way to an interior of marble counters, stained-glass windows, gleaming brass and ornately carved 'snugs'. The way to call for service is to use the antique system of bell pulls. Since it was built in 1839, the saloon, still lit by gas mantles, has developed its own folklore, including a story of it being linked by underground tunnels to the Opera House across the road.

ULSTER MUSEUM ✪✪✪

In the lovely surroundings of the Botanic Garden, the Ulster Museum gives a fascinating insight into the life and history of the Province. Collections include antiquities, art, botany, zoology, geology, technology, glass, silver and Irish furniture, and there are a number of permanent themed exhibitions. 'Made in Belfast' underlines the industry and inventiveness of Ulster (Northern Ireland) people, and there are displays on dinosaurs, armada treasures, the flora and fauna of Ireland and 'Early Ireland'.

76B2
Donegall Square
01232 320202 ext 227
Guided tours available if booked in advance
Free

76A1
Botanic Avenue
01232 320202 ext 3439
Park: daily 8–dusk;
Palmhouse: Mon–Fri
10–12 1–5, Sat–Sun 1–5
See Ulster Museum
84, 85
Botanic Station
Good
Free

76A2
Great Victoria Street
01232 249476
Licensing hours
Typically Irish dishes
Few
Free

76A1
Botanic Gardens
01232 383000
Mon–Fri 10–5, Sat 1–5,
Sun 2–5
Cafeteria (£)
69, 70, 71
Botanic Station
Good
Free

A Walk Around Belfast

This walk starts in the heart of the city, then heads south along 'The Golden Mile' to visit the lovely Botanic Gardens and the splendid Ulster Museum.

Donegall Square is surrounded by splendid architecture. Take a look at some of the statues and monuments in the grounds of City Hall before going inside (guided tours can be arranged in advance).

Leave by the exit on the opposite side. Outside the gates of City Hall turn left along Donegall Square South. At the corner cross into May Street, then turn right into Alfred Street. Continue to reach St Malachy's on the left.

St Malachy's was built in 1844 in castellated Gothic style with dark red brick and slender octagonal turrets. Inside there is fine fan-vaulting and an organ by Telford.

From St Malachy's go forward into Clarence Street, turn left into Bedford Street, then bear right into Dublin Street and continue to Shaftesbury Square. Continue along Bradbury Place and fork left into University Road. Beyond the university, turn left to enter the Botanic Gardens, where the Ulster Museum can be found.

The beautiful Botanic Gardens feature a great Palm House and Tropical Ravine. Near by is the excellent Ulster Museum.

Retrace your steps to Shaftesbury Square, then fork left to go along Great Victoria Street, passing the Crown Liquor Saloon on the right.

Try to time the walk so that this famous National Trust pub, with its sumptuous and ornate Victorian interior, will be open.

Continue past the Europa Hotel and the splendid Opera House, then turn right into Howard Street and return to Donegall Square.

Distance
About 4km

Time
3–4 hours, including cathedral, garden and museum visits

Start/end point
Donegall Square
✚ 76B2
🚌 All city centre buses

Lunch
Crown Liquor Saloon (££)
✉ Great Victoria Street
☎ 01232 249476

The Crown Liquor Saloon is a wonderful piece of living history

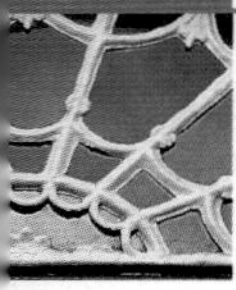

Splendidly imposing St Patrick's RC Cathedral contains the red hats of the cardinal archbishops of Armagh

What to See in The North

ARMAGH

Armagh is a distinguished city with a heritage of national importance. Nearby Navan Fort was the ancient capital of the Kings of Ulster, and in AD 445 St Patrick built his first church on the site now occupied by St Patrick's Cathedral. From here the Irish were converted to Christianity and Armagh remains the ecclesiastical capital of Ireland. There has been much rebuilding of this Church of Ireland cathedral, but its core is medieval. There is also a Roman Catholic cathedral of St Patrick, finished in 1904, with a lavish interior of murals depicting Irish saints. **St Patrick's Trian**, in English Street, has an exhibition on the saint.

> ### Did you know ?
>
> *St Patrick was born about AD 390 in Britain, the son of a Romano-British official. At 16 he was kidnapped by pirates and sold into slavery in Ireland, but later escaped with, he claimed, divine intervention. This prompted his training for the ministry in Britain, before returning to Ireland and establishing the Christian faith there.*

The city has many other beautiful buildings in delightful old streets, and the stables of the former Archbishop's Palace has been converted into an excellent **Heritage Centre**. Armagh looks to the future too, with its famous **Planetarium**, which offers much more than a star show.

BALLYCASTLE

Ballycastle, Co Antrim's largest town, is a popular seaside resort surrounded by some of Ireland's loveliest scenery. Near by is the Carrick-a-Rede rope bridge, suspended

---

Sidebar (left column):

75C2
From Portadown Station
Portadown

St Patrick's Trian
40 English Street
01861 521801
Apr–Sep, Mon–Sat 10–6, Sun 1–6 (till 5 Oct–Mar)
Restaurant (£)
Good
Moderate

Heritage Centre
The Palace Demesne
01861 529629
Apr–Sep, Mon–Sat 10–6, Sun 1–6; Oct–Mar, Mon–Sat 10–5, Sun 2–5
Coffee shop (£); restaurant (£)
Good
Moderate

Planetarium
College Hill
01861 523689
Mon–Fri 10–4:45, Sat–Sun 1:15–4:45
Coffee shop, snack bar (£)
Good
Expensive

75D3
From Ballymoney Station
Ballymoney

24.5m above the sea, linking the clifftop to a rocky island, and from the harbour there are trips to Rathlin Island, one of the best places for birdwatching in Ireland. On the edge of the town are the ruins of **Bonamargy Friary**, founded

around 1500 and the burial place of the MacDonnell chiefs. At the end of August each year, the Diamond at the centre of the town is crammed with the stalls, entertainments and horse dealing of the famous Oul' Lammas Fair. **The Ballycastle Museum** is housed in the 18th-century courthouse, and there is a Seafront Exhibition Centre with crafts and information.

Bonamargy Friary
✉ Ballycastle
☎ 01232 235000
🕐 All year
♿ Few
💷 Free

Ballycastle Museum
✉ Castle Street
☎ 012657 62942
🕐 Jul–Aug, daily 12–6
♿ None
💷 Free

Intrepid visitors cross the Carrick-a-Rede rope bridge

CARRICKFERGUS ✪✪

Carrickfergus has the country's finest Norman **castle**, constructed on the edge of the sea in the late 12th century and still in use (as a magazine and armoury) as recently as 1928. Its impressive walls now house three floors of exhibitions and a medieval fair is held here each July.

There are remains of the 17th-century town walls, the earliest and largest urban defence in Ulster, including the North Gate which has been rebuilt and restored.

Carrickfergus was the first footfall in Ireland of William of Orange, who landed at the harbour in 1690 for his victorious campaign against James II. Billy's Rock reputedly marks the exact spot.

Bringing the town right up to the minute is **Knight Ride**, a hi-tech centre which carries visitors on a monorail excursion through the ages.

➕ 75D2
🚍 Belfast–Larne
🚆 Carrickfergus

Carrickfergus Castle
✉ Marine Highway
☎ 01960 351273
🕐 Apr–Sep, Mon–Sat 10–6, Sun 2–6; Oct–Mar, Mon–Sat 10–4, Sun 2–4
♿ Few 💷 Moderate

Knight Ride
✉ Antrim Street
☎ 01960 366455
🕐 Mon–Sat 10–6, Sun 12–6
♿ Good 💷 Moderate

DONEGAL ✪✪

Donegal Tweed has made the name of this northwest corner of Ireland familiar all around the world. It is a modest little town, but it has the remains of two castles and two abbeys, and is attractively set at the head of Donegal Bay. **Donegal Castle**, on the banks of the River Eask in the town centre, was built in 1505 for Red Hugh O'Donnell and was considerably enlarged in the 17th century for Sir Basil Brooke. The Brooke family also owned Lough Eask Castle, a Jacobean-style house which suffered from a fire in 1939.

South of the town is **Donegal Abbey**. Here, in the 17th century, *The Annals of the Four Masters*, was written, charting the history of Ireland up until 1616. This important chronicle is now in the National Library in Dublin (▶ 34).

➕ 74A2

Donegal Castle
✉ Tinchonaill Street
☎ 073 22405
🕐 Mid-June–mid-Sep 10–6
🍴 Refreshments
💷 Cheap

Donegal Abbey
✉ Donegal
🕐 Daily
🍴 Refreshments

81

In the Know

If you only have a short time to visit Ireland, or would like to get a real flavour of the country, here are some ideas:

10
Ways To Be A Local

Relax – the local saying is that God created time, then he gave the Irish more of it.

Talk – strike up conversation wherever you go. No Irish person would walk into an occupied room without saying something to someone.

Do not take things too seriously – the Irish are renowned for their sense of humour and storytelling.

Develop a taste for Guinness – it somehow makes you feel you belong. And be patient – it takes a long time to pour a good pint.

Be subtle – the Irish tend not to be loud and brash, so make your enquiries soft and your conversation easy.

Be geniune – the Irish are usually really interested in what you have to say.

Know how to let your hair down – that laid-back attitude seems to evaporate when the time comes to have a 'hooley'.

Forget the old Hollywood myths and stereotypes – there may be a degree of unsophistication in the rural areas, but the Irish are generally outward-looking and forward-thinking.

Do not mind the weather – though Ireland has a mild climate, there is a strong possibility that you will be rained on at some point. Head for a cosy bar and wait for the sun to reappear.

Forget your diet – the Irish know how to fill a plate, particularly at breakfast time, and it all tastes too good to pass up.

10
Good Places To Have Lunch

Ahernes (£) ✉ 163 North Main Street, Youghal, Co Cork ☎ 024-92424. Plenty of awards have been won by this charming restaurant.

Ballymaloe House (££) ✉ Shanagarry Midleton, Co Cork ☎ 021-652431. You could hardly fail to get a good lunch here, at the home of the Ballymaloe Cookery School. Local produce is used to full advantage to produce excellent, good-value food.

Dunraven Arms (££) ✉ On the edge of the village, Adare, Co Limerick ☎ 061-396633. A lovely old country inn in one of Ireland's prettiest villages.

Gallagher's Boxty House (£) ✉ 20–1 Temple Bar, Dublin ☎ 01-6772762 Traditional Irish food, including boxties and champ, is the speciality of this well-established Temple Bar restaurant.

Harvey's Point (££) ✉ Lough Eask, Donegal ☎ 073-22208. Wonderful food in a wonderful location on the edge of Lough Eske.

Hooker Jimmy's Steak and Seafood Bar (££) ✉ The Fishmarket, Spanish Arch, Galway ☎ 091-568351. Right by the Spanish Arch, offers well-cooked dishes, particularly seafood and oysters.

Patrick Guilbaud (£££) ✉ 46 James Place, off Lower Baggot Street, Dublin ☎ 01-6764192. One of the finest restaurants in the city offering superb classic French cuisine in elegant surroundings. Popular with business clients.

Ramore Restaurant, ✉ The Harbour Portrush, Co Antrim ☎ 01265-824313. A popular restaurant right on the harbour. offering excellent food and a good wine list.

Roscoff Restaurant (£££)
✉ 7 Lesley House, Shaftesbury Square, Belfast
☎ 01232-331532. TV chef Paul Rankin and his wife run this city centre restaurant of high repute.

Savannagh Restaurant (££) ✉ Trident Hotel, World's End, Kinsale
☎ 021-772301. Award-winning restaurant overlooking the harbour.

Top Activities

- Angling
- Birdwatching
- Cruising on the Shannon or Erne waterways
- Cycling
- Going to a pub music session
- Golf
- Horse-racing
- Horse-riding
- Sailing
- Walking

Boat Trips

Athlone–Clonmacnoise (Booking office, Rossana Cruises, Crannagh, Galway Road, Athlone, Co Westmeath)

Cork Harbour from Cobh (Booking office Marine Transport Services, Atlantic Quay, Cobh)

Dingle Bay and Fungi the Dolphin (Booking office, Dingle Bay Ferries, Dunromen, Lispole, Co Kerry)

Killarney Lakes from Ross Castle (Booking office, Killarney Watercoach Cruises, 3 High Street, Killarney, Co Kerry)

Lough Corrib and Inchagoill Island (Booking office, Tourist office, Eyre Square, Galway)

Lough Derg–Killaloe (Booking office, Derg

Maine, Kilaloe, Co Clare)

Lough Key Forest Park (Booking office, Lough Key Boat Tours, Lakeshore Restaurant, Lough Key Forest Park, Boyle, Co Roscommon)

Lough Ree–Athlone (Booking office, Shannon Holidays, Jolly Mariner, Maine, Athlone, Co Westmeath)

River Erne from Belturbet (Booking office, Tarbot Tours, Deanery Park, Belturbet, Co Cavan)

Waterford–Carrick-on-Suir Castle (Booking office, Gallery Cruising Restaurant, Bridge Quay, New Ross, Co Wexford)

Souvenir Ideas

- Aran Knitwear
- Belleek Pottery
- Claddagh Rings
- Connemara Marble
- Donegal Tweed
- Irish Linen
- Irish Whiskey
- Limerick Lace
- Peat Carvings
- Waterford Crystal

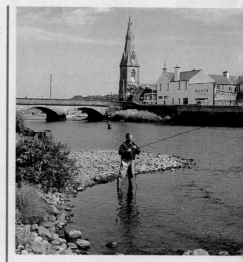

Ballina, in Co Mayo, is a popular angling centre

Events

- Pan Celtic Festival, Galway, Co Galway. April.
- International Folk Dance Festival, Cobh, Co Cork. July.
- Oul' Lammas Fair, Ballycastle, Co Antrim. August.
- Ballyshannon International Folk Festival, Co Donegal. August.
- Rose of Tralee Festival, Tralee, Co Kerry. August.
- Galway International Oyster Festival, Co Galway. September.
- Storytelling Festival, Cape Clear, Co Cork. September.
- Kinsale Gourmet Festival, Co Cork. October.
- Wexford Opera Festival, Wexford, October.
- Belfast Arts Festival, November.

83

☐ 74B2
⛴ Ferry from Lower Lough Erne, 5km north of Enniskillen, to Devenish Island

Enniskillen Castle
⊠ Castle Barracks
☎ 01365 325000
⏲ Mon 2–5, Tue–Fri 10–5. Also open Sat 2–5 from May–Sep and Sun 2–5 in Jul & Aug
🍴 Snacks (£)
🚌 Ulster Bus Station
♿ Few **🚍** Cheap

Castle Coole
☎ 01365 322690
⏲ Easter, Apr & Sep, weekends & bank hols; May–Aug, daily 1–6 (last tour 5:15). Closed Thu
🍴 Refreshments (£)
🚌 95 from Enniskillen
♿ Few **🚍** Moderate

Florence Court
☎ 01365 348249
⏲ Easter, daily 1–6; Apr & Sep, weekends and bank hols 1–6; May–Aug, daily 1–6. Closed Tue
🍴 Tea room (£)
🚌 Ulsterbus 192 Enniskillen–Swanlinbar
♿ Few **🚍** Moderate

☐ 75C3

Dunluce Castle
⊠ A2, east of Portrush
☎ 012657-31938

ENNISKILLEN ☻☻

Enniskillen is attractively set on the River Erne between Upper and Lower Lough Erne. **Enniskillen Castle**, built in early 15th century, was the medieval stronghold of the Maguires and has a picturesque water gate. The keep now houses the Fermanagh Museum and a military museum. St Macartan's Cathedral is a small but interesting building, dating from the early 17th century, with some fine monuments and stained glass.

The Fermanagh Lakelands surrounding Enniskillen provide for all kinds of water-based leisure pursuits, and on Devenish Island is an important monastic site, founded in the 6th century by St Molaise.

A little further afield is **Castle Coole**, a fine neo-classical house designed by James Wyatt in 1795. The interiors are exquisite and the lovely parkland runs down to the shores of Lough Coole. **Florence Court** is to the southwest, a fine 18th-century mansion noted for its plasterwork.

Florence Court is magnificently set in mature parkland, part of which is now a Forest Park

THE GIANT'S CAUSEWAY (► 20–1, TOP TEN)

THE GIANT'S CAUSEWAY COAST ☻☻

The Giant's Causeway coast encompasses dramatic cliffs, wide sandy beaches, pretty fishing villages and clifftop castles. Portrush, the nearest large town, is a traditional seaside resort with two splendid beaches, and near by is **Dunluce Castle**, a fairytale ruin which seems to grow out of the rock on which it is perched. Portballintrae is a pretty fishing village, made famous by the discovery in 1967 of the most valuable sunken treasure ever found on an armada wreck – the *Girona* – which foundered here in 1588, with only five survivors from its 1,300 crew. The rescued treasure is now on display and can be seen in Belfast's Ulster Museum.

Apr–Sep, Mon–Sat 10–7, Sun 2–7; Oct–Mar, Tue–Sat 10–4, Sun 2–4

172 Portrush–Ballycastle

Cheap

William Thackeray described beautiful Glenariff as 'Switzerland in miniature'

THE GLENS OF ANTRIM ✪✪✪

There are nine Glens of Antrim, lying roughly east of an imaginary line drawn between Ballycastle and Ballymena, and all of them are beautiful. There are wide valleys with a patchwork of green pastures, densely wooded mountain slopes and rocky gorges with tumbling streams dappled by the sunlight shining through the overhanging trees. Many of the glens are designated nature reserves and there are splendid walks, rich in wildlife and botanical interest and often with views to the coast. Millions of years of geological upheaval have formed these delightful valleys, which lie between the great plateau of the Antrim Mountains and a coastline that is justifiably described as the most scenic in the British Isles (➤ 90). Glenariff, the best known, has been dubbed the 'queen of the glens', and there is a wonderful view from the visitor centre.

75C3/75D3

Tourist Information Centre: Sheskburn House, 7 Mary Street, Ballycastle (☎ 012657 62024/62225)

LETTERKENNY ✪

Letterkenny is on the River Swilly, with the lovely Fanad and Inishowen peninsulas to the north, and the Glenveagh National Park and Derryveagh Mountains to the west.

Letterkenny's long main street is overlooked by the Cathedral of St Eunan, built around 100 years ago and containing some important stained glass. The Donegal County Museum has artefacts from the Stone Age to medieval periods as well as more recent history and folk life. In Church Hill, on the shore of Lough Gartan, the lovely **Glebe House** is now an art gallery, and just outside the town on the Kilmacrenan road is Brian McGee Pottery.

74B3

Glebe House and Gallery

✉ Church Hill

☎ 074-37071

Easter & mid-May–late Sep, 11–6:30. Closed Fri

Tea room (£)

Good

Cheap

Londonderry's Victorian Guildhall towers over Shipquay Street

✚ 74B3

Tower Museum
✉ Union Hall Place
☎ 01504 372411
🕐 Jul–Aug, Mon–Sat 10–5, Sun 2–5; Sep–Jun, Tue– Sat 10–5
🚉 Londonderry
♿ Good
💷 Moderate

LONDONDERRY ⚫⚫

Londonderry is a city that is historically absorbing, yet lively and modern too, with lots of festivals, events and entertainments. The perfect introduction is to take a guided walk of about 1.5km around its 17th-century town walls, which are still unbroken in spite of a 105-day siege by Jacobite forces in 1689, one of the most significant battles in Irish history. The city had hardly ever been trouble-free. Ever since St Columba founded his first monastery here in AD 546, its strategic and accessible location on the Foyle estuary attracted marauders. The complete story is told in the award-winning **Tower Museum**.

> ### *Did you know ?*
>
> *The English forces, who took the city of Derry in the mid–16th century, accidentally blew up most of the medieval city when their munitions exploded. The subsequent rebuilding was carried out (somewhat unwillingly) by the City of London Guilds, hence the 'London' prefix. To this day many people still adhere to the city's original name of Derry.*

Londonderry has impressive public buildings, two fine cathedrals and dramatic townscapes, but there are also lots of little lanes to explore, and behind the 19th-century Guildhall is the quay from which so many emigrants sailed for the New World.

✚ 75C2

LOUGH NEAGH ⚫

Lough Neagh, the largest lake in the British Isles, has little hidden harbours, sandy beaches and a number of islands.

Lakes are always best explored by boat, and this one is no exception, because the roads around it rarely follow the waterline. The *Maid of Antrim* cruises around the lake from the marina at Antrim, a busy and attractive town, with a famous 9th-century round tower. Nearby **Shane's Castle** looks out over the water and a narrow-gauge steam railway runs along the shore. Away from the noise of the locomotives, there are birdwatching hides and a nature trail.

In the southeastern corner of the lough, Oxford Island has a range of habitats for birdlife, including wet meadows, reedbeds, woodlands and shoreline scrub. The **Lough Neagh Discovery Centre** here has computer simulations, an Ecolab and birdwatching hides.

THE MOUNTAINS OF MOURNE ✪✪

Percy French wrote many popular songs extolling the beauty of Ireland, but his best-known line must surely be '*where the Mountains of Mourne sweep down to the sea*'. Few first-time visitors, though, would be prepared for the wild beauty of the scenery.

The **Mourne Countryside Centre** at Newcastle is a good place to start, with lots of information and guided walks. One of the nature trails follows the 'Brandy Pad', a notorious smugglers' route that links Hilltown, appropriately notable for its many pubs, with the coast south of Newcastle.

Slieve Donard, at 839m, is the highest mountain, and clothing its slopes is the Donard Forest Park. There is more woodland in the Tollymore and Castlewellan Forest Parks, while to the south is the evocatively named Silent Valley, flooded to form two great reservoirs. There is a charge for cars to enter the forest parks and Silent Valley, which is accessible from about 10AM (closing time varies depending on the season).

Shane's Castle
- ✉ A6 west of Antrim
- ☎ 01849 463380/428216
- ⏲ Telephone for details
- ♿ Good 🚻 Moderate

Lough Neagh Discovery Centre
- ✉ Oxford Island
- ☎ 01762 322205
- ⏲ Apr–Sep, daily 10–7; Oct–Mar, Wed–Sun 10–5
- 🍴 Cafe (££)
- 🚌 Ulsterbus 52 from Lurgan
- ♿ Good 🚻 Moderate

➕ 75D1

Mourne Countryside Centre
- ✉ 91 Central Promenade, Newcastle
- ☎ 013967 24059
- ⏲ May–Sep, Mon–Fri 9–5, Sat & Sun 12–5
- ♿ Few
- 🚻 Free

Newcastle nestles beneath the beautiful Mountains of Mourne

Greyabbey Road, Newtownards

House: May–Sep daily, plus Easter week, weekends Apr & Oct; Gardens: Apr–Sep daily, weekends Mar & Oct.

Coffee shop (£)

Ulsterbus 9 & 10 from Newtownards

Bangor

Good　Moderate

MOUNT STEWART HOUSE AND GARDENS ✪✪✪

One of Ireland's grandest stately homes, Mount Stewart was built for the 3rd Marquess of Londonderry. Three architects were involved in the building – James Wyatt, in the 1780s, then George Dance and (probably) William Vitruvious Morrison in the early 19th century. The imposing interior largely reflects the impeccable taste of the 7th Marchioness, a leader of London society in the 1920s and 1930s. She was also responsible for the beautiful garden, among the very best in the care of the National Trust, which benefits from the mild climate between the Irish Sea and Strangford Lough.

ULSTER AMERICAN FOLK PARK (► 26, TOP TEN)

75D2

Bangor Road, Cultra, Holywood

01232 428428

Apr–Jun & Sep, Mon–Fri 9:30–5, Sat 10:30–6, Sun 12–6; Jul–Aug, Mon–Sat 10:30–6, Sun 12–6; Oct–Mar, Mon–Fri 9:30–4, Sat and Sun 12:30–4:30. Closed Christmas

Tea room (£)

Belfast–Bangor route

Cultra Halt

Few　Moderate

ULSTER FOLK AND TRANSPORT MUSEUM ✪✪

All kinds of Ulster buildings have been painstakingly dismantled in their original locations, brought to this 55.5-hectare site and reconstructed in authentic settings, including a small town of the 1900s, complete with shops, a school, churches, printer's workshops, a bank and terraced houses. Rural exhibits include traditional Irish cottages, watermills and farmhouses, and farming is represented by rare breeds of animals and fields which are cultivated using traditional methods.

The Transport Museum is very comprehensive, covering all forms of transport from horse-drawn carts to the De Lorean car, and includes the superb Irish Railway Collection, aircraft and ships. Perennially popular is the *Titanic* exhibition, on the 'unsinkable' liner which was built

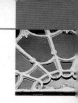

in Belfast's shipyards and foundered after hitting an iceberg on her maiden voyage.

As well as the permanent exhibitions and buildings, the museum has lots of special events, which change from year to year.

A fine old kitchen at the Ulster Folk Museum

THE ULSTER HISTORY PARK

This is another museum of reconstructed dwellings, farmsteads and fortifications, but it delves right back into prehistoric times, to the time of the earliest settlers in Ireland. There is a mesolithic encampment of the kind that would have been inhabited in the period 8000–4000 BC. From here we travel through the ages, with the houses and megalithic tombs of the early farmers of 4000–2200 BC, a ring fort, and a *crannog*. These settlements were built on artificial islands in lakes for defensive purposes and were surrounded by a brushwood pallisade. The historical tour continues with a medieval monastic settlement, complete with round tower, and a Norman motte-and-bailey castle. Finally there is a Plantation settlement of the 17th century.

These full-size replicas, constructed using authentic methods and materials, trace the progress of living conditions through the ages, and the excellent visitor centre explains the significance of each of the buildings. The museum hosts a number of demonstrations, special events and festivals throughout the year.

+ 74B2
✉ Cullion
☎ 016626 48188
⊙ Apr–Sep, Mon–Sat 10:30–6:30, Sun 11:30–7, bank hols 10:30–7; Oct–Mar, Mon–Fri 10:30–5 (last admission 1½ hours before closing)
🍴 Cafeteria (£)
🚌 Omagh–Gortin route
♿ Few
✋ Moderate

The Spectacular Antrim Coast

Distance
160km

Time
About 7 hours

Start/end point
Larne
✚ 75D3

Lunch
Wysner's (£)
✉ 16 Ann Street,
   Ballycastle
☎ 012657 62372

From Larne take the A2 north signed Glenarm and the Antrim Coast Road.

All the way to Ballycastle there is wonderful coastal scenery and pretty villages. Turn off to explore the Glens of Antrim if you have time.

Pass Bonamargy Friary on the left and at the T-juction turn left into Ballycastle. From the Diamond take the A2 signposted 'Portrush, Bushmills, Giant's Causeway'. Soon turn right, signposted 'Ballintoy, B15, Coastal Route'. At the T-junction turn right and continue, passing the turning to Carrick-a-Rede Rope Bridge.

In summer the rope bridge is strung high above the water across the gap between the mainland and a little rocky island.

Go through Ballintoy and after 5.6km turn right into Causeway Road. after another 5.6km reach the Visitor Centre.

This is a World Heritage Site and a unique phenomenon which should not be missed.

Spectacular scenery at Glenarm on the Antrim Coast Road

From the Causeway, take the A2 to Bushmills and at the roundabout in the village go straight on, signposted 'Dervock'. After a short distance, reach the Bushmills Distillery on the left.

Though it is a large-scale working distillery, Bushmills is well geared up for visitors, with an interesting and entertaining tour, tastings and shops.

Continue to Dervock, then at T-junction turn right with the B66, signposted 'Ballymoney'. About 6.4km further on turn left on to the A26. Keep on this road and at the end of its short motorway section, reach a roundabout and turn left. From here follow signs back to Larne.

Where To...

Above: *Folk music at
Bailey's Corner, Tralee*
Right: *Kilkenny pub sign*

The East

Prices

Approximate prices for a three-course meal for one person are shown by the pound symbol:

£ = budget   under £10
££ = moderate   £10–£20
£££= expensive   over £20

Black and White

Guinness developed from an 18th-century beer called porter because it was brewed for the porters in London's Billingsgate market. The drink was brought to Ireland by Cork brewers, Beamish and Crawford, and became known as stout when Guinness increased its alcoholic content and sold it as 'extra stout porter'.

Carlingford
Co Louth

Jordan's Townhouse Restaurant (£–£££)

Overlooking the delightful harbour, this award-winning restaurant specialises in seafood, notably the fresh lobster from the tank.

✉ Newry Street ☎ 042-73223 ⏰ Mon–Sat for lunch & dinner. Closed Sun evening Nov–Christmas & last 3 weeks in Jan

Dalkey
Co Dublin

La Romana (££)

A number of best pub awards have been won by this colourful place, which serves good Italian cuisine.

✉ Castle Street ☎ 01-2854569 ⏰ Dinner only. Closed 25–6 Dec, Jan 1 & Good Fri

Dublin
Co Dublin

Dublin has an enormous variety of places to eat and drink, with every kind of international food available, and if you want to browse before deciding, there are certain areas in the city where restaurants are conveniently clustered. For lively and entertaining cafe-bars and cosmopolitan restaurants, head for Temple Bar; for more elegance and sophistication, look along Baggot Street and around Ballsbridge.

Fitzsimmons Bar & Restaurant (£)

A lively and welcoming bar/restaurant with Irish set dancing to entertain you while you eat.

✉ East Essex Street, Temple Bar ☎ 01-6779315 ⏰ Lunch, dinner

Patrick Guilbaud (£££)

First-class restaurant specialising in French cuisine. Lovely venue for special occasions.

✉ 21 Upper Merrion Street ☎ 01-6764192 ⏰ Lunch, dinner. Closed Sun & Mon

Periwinkle Seafood Bar (£)

This is a good place for a quick lunch break within the delightful Powerscourt Townhouse Shopping Centre. Seafood chowder is a speciality.

✉ Unit 18, Powerscourt Townhouse Centre, South William Street ☎ 01-6794203 ⏰ During shopping hours. Closed Sun & Bank hols

Longfield's (££)

The speciality of this fine restaurant is game, along with seafood and Mediterranean dishes.

✉ 9–10 Fitzwilliam Street Lower ☎ 01-6761367 ⏰ Lunch, dinner. Closed for lunch Sat & Sun

Foulkesmills
Co Wexford

Cellar Restaurant (££)

A restaurant full of character in a flag-stoned cellar of a country mansion.

✉ Horetown House ☎ 051-565771 ⏰ Dinner, Sun lunch. Closed Mon, except Bank hols, 3 days at Christmas

Glencullen
Co Dublin

Johnnie Fox's Pub (£)

Johnnie Fox's is known far and wide for its excellent seafood, with fresh mussels the speciality of the house. Traditional music and dancing nightly.

☎ 01-2955647 ⏰ Lunch, dinner. Closed Sun lunch, 25 Dec & Good Fri

Howth
Co Dublin
King Sitric Fish Restaurant (££)

Famous fish restaurant, which has won many awards.

✉ East Pier ☎ 01-8325235
🕐 Lunch, dinner. Closed Sun, bank hols & 2 weeks in Jan. Lunch not served Oct–Apr

Johnstown
Co Kildare
Johnstown Inn (££)

Traditional Irish food (and occasionally traditional Irish music) is on offer here, but the specialities are peppered steaks and prawns. The inn is situated on the attractive main street of the village.

✉ Northeast of Naas on the N7
☎ 045-897547 🕐 Daily for lunch & dinner. Closed 24–6 Dec, 1 Jan & Good Fri

Killiney
Co Dublin
Truffles Restaurant (££)

A number of awards have come the way of this restaurant in a converted castle overlooking Dublin Bay. Sole Bonne Femme is the speciality. The name is due to change during the currency of this guide.

✉ Fitzpatrick Castle Hotel
☎ 01-2840700 🕐 Daily for lunch & dinner

Kilkenny
Co Kilkenny
Kilkenny Design Centre (£)

The restaurant at this complex of craft workshops matches up to the quality Irish craft wares on sale here, with Irish traditional dishes and vegetarian selections on the menu.

✉ Castle Yard ☎ 056-22118
🕐 Daily during shopping hours. Closed Sun & Bank hols

Parliament House (££)

Traditional local dishes are the speciality of this charming restaurant, with some European dishes.

✉ Parliament Street
☎ 056-63666 🕐 Lunch, dinner

Laragh
Co Wicklow
Mitchell's (££)

An award-winning restaurant in the heart of the Wicklow Mountains, offering Irish and European dishes.

☎ 0404-45302 🕐 Lunch, dinner. Closed Mon & Tue in winter, 24–6 Dec, last 3 weeks in Jan & Good Fri

Malahide
Co Dublin
Bon Appetit (£££)

There is a first-class wine list to accompany the traditional Irish and seafood specialities here.

✉ 9 James Terrace
☎ 01-8450314 🕐 Lunch, dinner. Closed Sun & bank hol, closed for lunch on Sat

Moone
Co Kildare
Moone High Cross Inn (££)

This roadside pub has gained a good reputation for its food, and the speciality is Irish Stew.

✉ Bolton Hill ☎ 0507-24112
🕐 Lunch, dinner

Roundwood
Co Wicklow
Roundwood Inn (££)

A cosy pub which has won awards for its food and its wine list. Seafood, game and traditional Irish dishes feature on the menu.

✉ Roundwood ☎ 01-2818107/2818125 🕐 Daily for lunch & dinner. Closed 25 Dec & Good Fri

Famous Drinkers
Ireland's famous writers were also great drinkers and had their favourites among the city's old pubs. A literary pub-crawl takes you around the most famous of them, with professional actors performing from the works of Joyce, O'Casey, Yeats, Behan et al. Tickets are available from the tourist office.

The South

Floating Food

Cruising restaurants ply the waters of the Rivers Barrow and Nore from New Ross and Waterford, offering a wonderfully relaxing way to eat and enjoy the scenery at the same time. The *St Ciaran* and the *St Brendan* can carry 70 or 80 diners. Lunch, afternoon tea and dinner cruises are all available, April to October. Booking is essential.

The Galley Cruising Restaurants
⊠ Bridge Quay, New Ross
☎ 051-21723

Adare
Co Limerick
Dunraven Arms (££)

This is a delightful country inn with an award-winning restaurant.
☎ 061-396633 ⏱ All year for lunch & dinner

Ballingarry
Co Limerick
The Mustard Seed (£££)

A pleasant drive through the Limerick countryside on quiet lanes leads to this first class restaurant in a stylish country house.
⊠ Echo Lodge ☎ 069-68508
⏱ Dinner only. Closed Sun in winter, 24–6 Dec, 1 Jan & whole of Feb

Baltimore
Co Cork
Chez Youen (££–£££)

This is among the best fish restaurants in Ireland. Drive up to the Beacon afterwards for wonderful views over the bay.
⊠ The Pier ☎ 028-20136
⏱ Easter–Sep lunch & dinner; dinner only in winter, except Sun. Closed Feb

La Jolie Brise (£)

This cheerful pizzeria, under the same management as Chez Youen, also offers fish and steak dishes on its menu.
⊠ The Pier ☎ 028-20441
⏱ All year, all day

Bantry
Co Cork
O'Connor's Seafood Restaurant (££)

Fresh local fish and shellfish are the specialities here.
⊠ The Square ☎ 027-50011
⏱ Lunch, dinner. Winter: closed Sun. Summer: closed Sun lunch

Cork
Co Cork
Café Mexicana (£)

Authentic Mexican cuisine and really good pizzas are served all day.
⊠ 1 Carey's Lane
☎ 021-276433 ⏱ Lunch, dinner

Crawford Art Gallery (££)

Excellent Irish and Mediterranean dishes served in Cork's superb art gallery.
⊠ Emmet Place
☎ 021-274415 ⏱ Lunch. Closed Sun

Dingle
Co Kerry
Doyle's Seafood Bar (££)

Fresh local fish and shellfish are served in this well-known bar.
⊠ John Street ☎ 066-51174
⏱ Dinner. Closed Sun & mid-Nov–mid-Mar

Lord Baker's (££)

Fish, game and succulent steaks are the speciality of this award-winning restaurant.
⊠ Main Street ☎ 066-51131
⏱ Lunch, dinner. Closed 24–6 Dec

Dunmore East
Co Waterford
The Ship (£)

Wonderful fresh lobster and prawns, French and Irish dishes are served in this charming pub.
☎ 051-383141 ⏱ Lunch, dinner. Oct–May: closed Sun & Mon. May & Sep: closed for lunch

Durrus
Co Cork
Blairs Cove Restaurant (£££)

Grills on an open wood fire

are the speciality of this restaurant.

☎ 027-61127 ⏰ Dinner. Closed Sun & Mon (but open Mon Jul & Aug) & Nov–Mar

Kenmare
Co Kerry
D'Arcy's (££)

French and Irish dishes can be enjoyed in this elegant restaurant.

✉ Main Street ☎ 064-41589 ⏰ Lunch, dinner. Closed Mon & first 2 weeks Feb

Killarney
Co Kerry
Foley's Seafood and Steak Restaurant (££)

The name says it all, and the restaurant is famous for it.

✉ 23 High Street ☎ 064-31217 ⏰ Lunch, dinner. Closed 24–6 Dec & lunchtime in winter

Gaby's Seafood Restaurant (££)

Lobster is the speciality in this attractive restaurant.

✉ 27 High Street ☎ 064-32519 ⏰ Lunch, dinner. Closed Sun

The Strawberry Tree (£££)

Sample the delights of New Ireland cuisine here.

✉ 24 Plunkett Street ☎ 064-32688 ⏰ Lunch by arrangement, dinner. Closed Dec & Jan

Kinsale
Co Cork
Chez Jean-Marc (££)

This fine restaurant offers imaginative French cooking, including excellent fresh seafood.

✉ Lower O'Connell Street ☎ 021-774625 ⏰ Dinner. Closed mid-Feb–mid-May & Mon until Jun

Max's Wine Bar (£)

Seafood and European dishes are complemented by an excellent wine list.

✉ Main Street ☎ 021-772443 ⏰ Lunch, dinner. Closed Nov–Feb

Limerick
Co Limerick
Freddy's Bistro (££)

This restaurant, serving Irish and Continental dishes is full of character.

✉ Theatre Lane, Lower Glentworth Street ☎ 061-418749 ⏰ Dinner. Closed Mon

Quenelle's Restaurant (£££)

Modern Irish cuisine is the speciality of this highly regarded restaurant.

✉ Sir Henry's, Mallow Street ☎ 061-411111 ⏰ Dinner. Closed Sun, Mon, Good Fri & 25 Dec

M J Finnegans (£)

One of Ireland's top pubs, offering seafood, steaks and Irish dishes.

✉ Dublin Road ☎ 061-337338 ⏰ Lunch, dinner. Closed Good Fri & 25 Dec

Schull
Co Cork
The Altar (££)

Delightful restaurant serving excellent fresh produce.

✉ Toormore ☎ 028-35254 ⏰ Lunch, dinner. Closed Oct–Mar (except New Year) & Sun

Waterford
Co Waterford
The Wine Vault (£)

A warm and cosy wine bar specialising in seafood.

✉ High Street ☎ 051-53444 ⏰ Lunch, dinner. Closed Sun, Good Fri & 25 Dec

Courses for Cooks

Surrounded by the lush countryside of Co Cork, the Ballymaloe Cookery School is internationally renowned. It offers a range of courses for all abilities, from complete novices to professionals, from a single day to a 12-week course, and the school's own kitchen gardens provide superb ingredients to work with. The school is run by Tim and Darina Allen, who have created a lovely informal atmosphere.

The West

Oysters

One of the most popular images of Irish cuisine is the plate of oysters and pint of Guinness, and there is nowhere better to sample the two together than at the Galway International Oyster Festival in September. Oysters are only eaten when there is an 'r' in the month, so this festival marks the beginning of the season and is a wonderful gastronomic celebration, accompanied by non-stop entertainment.

Aran Islands
Co Galway

Dun Aonghusa (££)

Irish and Continental dishes feature on the menu here, and the lobster is specially recommended.

✉ Kilronan, Inis Mór (Inishmore) ☎ 099 61104
🕐 Dinner. Closed Nov–Mar

Fisherman's Cottage (£)

This charming little restaurant features fresh local seafood and traditional Irish dishes.

✉ Inishere ☎ 099-75073
🕐 Lunch, dinner. Closed Oct–Apr

Barna (Bearna)
Co Galway

Donnelly's (£–££)

West of Galway city, on the scenic coast road to Connemara, is this Pub of the Year award winner. The menu is varied, with European dishes as well as local seafood.

☎ 091-592487 🕐 Daily from noon. Closed 24–5 Dec & Good Fri

Bunratty
Co Clare

Durty Nelly's (££)

Right next to Bunratty Castle, this famous pub is full of character and serves a variety of food in its cosy alcoves. Be prepared for crowds at the height of the tourist season.

☎ 061-364861 🕐 Lunch, dinner. Closed 25 Dec & Good Fri

Cashel, Co Galway

Cashel House Hotel (££)

Connemara lamb and other fresh local produce features on the menus at this lovely country house restaurant.

✉ Off N59, 1.5km west of Recess ☎ 095-31001
🕐 Lunch, dinner. Closed mid-Jan–mid-Feb

Clarenbridge
Co Galway

Paddy Burke's (£)

Famous as the focal point of the Clarenbridge Oyster Festival; no prizes for guessing the speciality dish.

☎ 091-796226 🕐 Lunch, dinner. Closed 25 Dec & Good Fri

Clifden
Co Galway

Ardagh Hotel and Restaurant (£££)

Award-winning restaurant offering European cuisine amidst wonderful Connemara scenery.

✉ Ballyconneely Road ☎ 095-21384 🕐 Dinner

Mitchell's (£)

Hearty Irish stew is the speciality of this attractive restaurant, with satisfying portions of seafood and steaks also on the menu.

✉ Market Street ☎ 095-21867
🕐 Lunch, dinner. Closed mid-Nov–mid-Mar

Collooney
Co Sligo

Markree Castle (££)

You can enjoy seafood, game and European dishes in magnificent surroundings at this historic castle hotel.

☎ 071-67800 🕐 Lunch, dinner

Cong
Co Mayo

Echoes (££)

Wild salmon, fresh and smoked is a speciality here, on a varied European menu.

✉ Main Street ☎ 092-46059
🕐 Lunch, dinner. Closed Mon–Thu from Nov–mid-Mar

Galway
Co Galway
Glenlo Abbey (£££)
High quality food is served in the modern wing of this restored 18th-century abbey.

✉ Bushypark, on the N59 ☎ 091-526666 🕐 Lunch, dinner

Hooker Jimmy's Steak and Seafood Bar (££)
The fresh lobster, scallops and oysters here are highly recommended.

✉ The Fishmarket, Spanish Arch ☎ 091-568351 🕐 Lunch, dinner. Closed 25–6 Dec

Sev'nth Heav'n (£)
Traditional Irish, Cajun and Mexican food is on offer in this lively little restaurant.

✉ Courthouse Lane ☎ 091-563838 🕐 Lunch, dinner. Closed 25–7 Dec

Stephan's Tigh Neachtain Restaurant (££)
Dishes from all over Europe feature on the menu of this city-centre restaurant.

✉ 2 Quay Street ☎ 091-846403 🕐 Dinner. Closed Sun, winter Mon & 2 weeks in Nov

Lisdoonvarna
Co Clare
The Orchid Restaurant (££)
Set in lovely gardens, this family-run hotel restaurant has won awards for food and hospitality.

✉ Sheedy's Spa View Hotel ☎ 065-74026 🕐 Dinner. Closed Oct–Apr

Moycullen
Co Galway
White Gables Restaurant (££)
This charming restaurant has a high reputation for its French cuisine and seafood.

☎ 091-85744 🕐 Lunch, dinner. Closed Mon in winter & 23 Dec–mid-Feb

Recess
Co Galway
Ballynahinch Castle (££)
Local game, fish and fresh local produce inspire the menus here.

✉ On Roundstone road, off N59, 5km west of Recess. ☎ 095-31006 🕐 Lunch, dinner. Closed 20–6 Dec & Feb

Rosses Point
Co Sligo
The Moorings (££)
A good variety of food is available at this pleasant pub in a very scenic area.

☎ 071-77112 🕐 Lunch, dinner. Closed Mon in winter

Sligo
Co Sligo
Embassy Restaurant (£–££)
Right in the heart of the town, this large restaurant has won awards for its bar food.

✉ John F Kennedy Parade ☎ 071-61250 🕐 Lunch, dinner. Closed 24–6 Dec & Good Fri

Westport
Co Mayo
Asgard Tavern (£)
One-time winner of Mayo Pub of the Year award, the Asgard offers well cooked seafood and Irish specialities.

✉ The Quay ☎ 098-25319 🕐 Lunch, dinner. Closed Sun & Mon off season

Quay Cottage (£)
Local shellfish and seafood are the speciality of this delightful little restaurant.

✉ The Harbour ☎ 098-26412 🕐 Lunch, dinner. Closed Christmas & Jan

Banquets
Irish medieval banquets are great fun, even if they are blatantly aimed at the tourist trade. Bunratty and Knappogue Castles are the most popular venues for these evenings of feasting in an authentic setting, with staff in medieval costume and traditional music.

The North

Afternoon Tea
National Trust tea rooms are well known for the quality of their cakes and scones, and those in Northern Ireland have the added benefit of the Ulster tradition of home baking. Recipes include an amazing variety of breads, potato cakes, soda breads, barm brack and biscuits. To round off a visit to one of the magnificent stately homes with afternoon tea is a real treat.

Throughout the Province of Northern Ireland look out for the green and white 'Taste of Ulster' sign, which guarantees the best of fresh, local produce.

Annalong
Co Down
Glassdrumman Lodge (£££)
Prime local produce, including prawns and salmon, feature on the 6-course dinner menu of well-produced dishes.
✉ 85 Mill Road ☎ 013967-68451 ⓘ Dinner

Ballycastle
Co Antrim
Wysner's (£)
Pleasant two-storey restaurant in the centre of town, with a range of reasonably priced dishes, including traditional Irish and a good selection of healthy eating options.
✉ 16 Ann Street ☎ 012657-62372 ⓘ Lunch, dinner. Closed Sun & winter Wed

Ballymena
Co Antrim
Galgorm Manor (£££)
The restaurant of this splendid 19th-century mansion offers modern Irish cooking with a French flavour.
☎ 01266-881001 ⓘ Lunch, dinner. Closed 24–6 Dec

Bangor
Co Down
Clandeboye Lodge Hotel (£)
Interesting treatment of good local produce in a secluded location.
✉ 10 Estate Road, Clandeboye ☎ 01247-852500 ⓘ Lunch, dinner. Closed 25–6 Dec

Deanes on the Square (££)
An imaginative menu of dishes cooked with flair and skill, within the stylish old railway building.
✉ 7 Station Square, Helen's Bay ☎ 01247-852841 ⓘ Lunch, dinner. Closed Sun dinner, Mon lunch & dinner, Christmas, New Year, 1 week in Jan & 1 week in Jul

Shanks (££)
Creative, contemporary cooking of a very high standard is offered in a light and airy restaurant.
✉ The Blackwood, Crawfordsburn Road ☎ 01247-853313 ⓘ Lunch, dinner. Closed Sun & Mon, 24–8 Dec & 2nd week in Jul

Belfast
In Belfast, the 'Golden Mile' between the Grand Opera House and Queen's University is the best place to search out restaurants, and the city-centre shopping areas have no shortage of coffee shops, fast food outlets and atmospheric pubs, such as the Crown Liquor Saloon.

Culloden Restaurant (£££)
Irish cooking with European influence in a charming mansion overlooking Belfast Lough.
✉ Bangor Road ☎ 01232-425223 ⓘ Lunch, dinner. Closed Sat lunch & 24—5 Dec

Rayanne Country House (££)
Small Victorian country house with interesting menu of dishes, with emphasis on flavour.
✉ 60 Desmesne Road ☎ 01232-425859 ⓘ Dinner. Closed Sun

Roscoff (£££)
Well-established city-centre restaurant with excellent reputation, run by TV chef Paul Rankin and his wife.
✉ **Lesley House, Shaftesbury Square** ☎ **01232-331532**
🕐 **Lunch, dinner. Closed Sat lunch, Sun lunch & dinner, 25–6 Dec & Easter Mon**

Saints and Scholars (£)
Lively restaurant in University area, specialising in seafood, game and European cuisine.
✉ **3 University Street** ☎ **01232-325137** 🕐 **Lunch, dinner. Closed Mon, Thu, 25 Dec & 12 Jul**

Skandia (£)
Warm and welcoming restaurant offering a variety of European and some Cajun dishes.
✉ **50 Howard Street** ☎ **01232-240239** 🕐 **Lunch, dinner. Closed Sun & 25–6 Dec**

Donegal
Co Donegal
St Ernan's House Hotel (£££)
On a lovely wooded island, reached by a causeway, this hotel restaurant has wonderful views and food.
✉ **3.2km south of Donegal on N15** ☎ **073-21065** 🕐 **Late Apr–late Oct for breakfast & dinner**

Hillsborough
Co Down
Hillside Restaurant and Bar (££)
Country-house cooking with global influences in this award-winning pub..
✉ **21 Main Street** ☎ **01846-682765** 🕐 **Lunch, dinner. Closed evenings of 25 Dec & Good Fri**

Inishowen
Co Donegal
Restaurant St John's (£££)
This is an award-winning restaurant which makes good use of the excellent local produce.
✉ **Fahan** ☎ **077-60289** 🕐 **Dinner. Closed Mon, Good Fri & 24–5 Dec**

Killyleagh
Co Down
Dufferin Arms (£–££)
The chef in this pleasant inn specialises in steaks, but also offers seafood and vegetarian choices.
✉ **35 High Street** ☎ **01396 828229** 🕐 **Mon–Sat, dinner only. Closed Sun**

Limavady
Co Londonderry
Radisson Roe Park Hotel (££)
Well-prepared dishes with a traditional French influence in a modern hotel.
☎ **015047-22222** 🕐 **Lunch, dinner**

Newtownabbey
Co Antrim
Sleepy Hollow Restaurant (£)
Charming little restaurant specialising in seafood and traditional Irish dishes.
✉ **15 Kiln Road** ☎ **01232-342042** 🕐 **Lunch, dinner. Closed Sun dinner**

Portaferry
Co Down
Portaferry Hotel (£££)
A charming 18th-century inn on the edge of Strangford Lough. The award-winning restaurant is best known for its seafood.
✉ **The Strand** ☎ **012477 28231** 🕐 **Daily for lunch, high tea & dinner. Closed 24–25 Dec**

Themed Foods
Special events at the Ulster American Folk Park near Omagh usually offer the chance to taste some kind of traditional delicacies, either of the Old Country or the New World. At the Frontier Festival Weekends in summer, guests can enjoy pioneer cooking, while at the end of October Halloween fare accompanies the dramatic antics around the park.

The East

Prices

Approximate prices for two people sharing a double room are shown by the pound symbol:

£ =   budget   under £40

££ = moderate £40–£80

£££= expensive over £80

The AA Hotel Booking Service

A new service exclusively for AA personal members.

A free, fast and easy way to find a place to stay for your short break, holiday or business trip.

With your AA membership number to hand, call and let us know your requirements. Our knowledgeable staff will help you make the right choice and book the accommodation for you.

0990 050505

"One call does it all"

Full listings of the British and Irish hotels and B&Bs available through the service can be found and booked at the AA's Internet site http://www.theaa.co.uk.hotels

Adare
Co Limerick
Adare Manor (£££)

An opulent hotel in a magnificent gothic mansion, surrounded by 340ha of parkland beside the River Maigue; including a championship golf course and other leisure facilities.

✉ On Killarney to Shannon route ☎ 061-396566 ⏰ Open all year

Avoca
Co Wicklow
Old Coach House (£)

A warm and inviting inn close to the Meeting of the Waters on the south-eastern edge of the Wicklow Mountains.

☎ 0402-35408

Cashel
Co Tipperary
Ros-guill House (£££)

An elegant and well-equipped country home overlooking the Rock of Cashel. Breakfasts here have won awards.

✉ On the Dualla road ☎ 062-61507 ⏰ Closed Nov–Apr

Dublin
Shelbourne Hotel (£££)

This famous and historic hotel overlooks St Stephen's Green in the heart of the city. It offers the ultimate in elegant and stylish accommodation.

✉ St Stephen's Green ☎ 01-6766471

Conrad International (£££)

Centrally located hotel offering excellent facilities and a choice of good restaurants.

✉ Earlsfort Terrace ☎ 01-6765555

Charleville Hotel (£)

This highly recommended guesthouse is in a Victorian terrace near Phoenix Park. The accommodation is of a very high standard and service is very friendly.

✉ 268–272 North Circular Road ☎ 01-8386633 ⏰ Closed 19–26 Dec

Gorey
Co Wexford
Marlfield House (£££)

Once the residence of the Earl of Courtown, this elegant and comfortable Regency house preserves an atmosphere of luxury.

☎ 055-21124 ⏰ Closed mid-Dec–end Jan

Kilkenny
Co Kilkenny
Swift's Heath (£)

This splendid country house and farm was once the home of Jonathan Swift, author of *Gulliver's Travels* and one-time dean of St Patrick's Cathedral in Dublin.

✉ Jenkinstown ☎ 056-67653 ⏰ Closed 21 Dec–end Jan

Rathnew
Co Wicklow
Tinakilly Country House (££)

This highly rated hotel is in an elegant mansion, peacefully set in three hectares of grounds, with sea views.

☎ 0404-69274

Straffan
Co Kildare
Kildare Hotel and Country Club (£££)

Sheer luxury and excellent food in magnificent suroundings. Facilities include a golf course and private fishing.

☎ 01-6273333

The South

Ballylickey
Co Cork
Sea View (££)
A delightful country house hotel overlooking Bantry Bay, with cosy and comfortable accommodation and very good food.
☎ 027-50073 & 50462

Bantry
Co Cork
Bantry House (££)
Enjoy good value bed and breakfast in style within one of Ireland's foremost stately homes.
✉ Cork Road ☎ 027-50047
🕐 Closed Nov–late Dec & Feb

Cork
Co Cork
Arbutus Lodge (££)
A period town house in a residential suburb, with a friendly atmosphere and smart surroundings.
✉ Middle Glanmire Road, Montenotte ☎ 021-501237

Kenmare
Co Kerry
Park Hotel (£££)
AA Hotel of the Year in 1997, the Park is synonymous with all the expectations of a luxury country-house hotel. It is on the Ring of Kerry, overlooking the estuary of the Kenmare River.
✉ On the R569 ☎ 064-41200

Sheen Falls Lodge (£££)
A luxury hotel with wonderful views of the cascading Sheen Falls.
☎ 064-41600 🕐 Closed Dec–early Feb, except Christmas and New Year

Killarney
Co Kerry
Aghadoe Heights (£££)
In a superb setting high above the Killarney Lakes, this hotel offers luxury and hospitality and an award-winning restaurant.
✉ 5km north of Killarney off N22 Tralee road ☎ 064-31766

Kinsale
Co Cork
Trident (££)
A harbour-side hotel with its own marina and boats for hire. There are superb views from many of the bedrooms.
✉ World's End ☎ 021-772301

Old Presbytery (£)
A charming period house on a quiet street in the town centre.
✉ 43 Cork Street ☎ 021-772027 🕐 Closed 24–8 Dec

Limerick
Co Limerick
Santolina (£)
Spacious and comfortable bed and breakfast accommodation in a modern bungalow within easy reach of the city.
✉ Coonagh, off the Ennis Road, 3km from city centre ☎ 061-451590 🕐 Closed Christmas

Mallow
Co Cork
Longueville House (£££)
An 18th-century mansion in a wooded estate, with elegant interior and excellent food.
✉ 5km west of Mallow on N72 ☎ 022-47156 & 47306

Waterford
Co Waterford
Waterford Castle (£££)
This ivy-clad castle stands on an island and retains many of its original features, including 16th-century oak panelling, stone walls and graceful arches.
✉ The Island ☎ 051-878203

Sporting Activities
Many visitors to Ireland come specifically to indulge in one of three sporting activities – angling, golf and horse riding. Hotels, guest houses and self-catering establishments have not been slow to recognise the demand, and a large number of them will make all the necessary arrangements for their guests to enjoy their chosen activity.

The West

Irish Kings
Clonalis House in Co Roscommon is the home of the O'Conors of Connacht, descendants of the Kings of Connacht and the last High King of Ireland, and it was built in Victorian times on land which has been owned by the family for 1,500 years. Guests here can browse through old family manuscripts and see the harp which belonged to the great Turlough O'Carolan.

✉ **On the west side of Castlerea on the N60**
☎ 0907-20014
🕐 **Closed Oct–mid-Apr (££)**

Ballynahinch
Co Galway
Ballynahinch Castle (£££)
Furnished with antiques, Ballynahinch Castle offers high standards of food and accommodation in the heart of Connemara.

✉ **Off the N59 5km from Recess**
☎ 095-31006 & 31086

Bunratty
Co Clare
Bunratty Lodge (£)
Highly recommended bed and breakfast in a spacious detached house; prize-winning breakfasts.

✉ **Between Bunratty Castle and Durty Nelly's** ☎ 061-369402 🕐 **Closed Nov–Feb**

Cashel
Co Galway
Cashel House (££)
Gracious country house hotel in award-winning gardens overlooking Cashel Bay. There is an atmosphere of luxury and peaceful elegance.

✉ **Off the N59, 1.5km west of Recess** ☎ 095-31001
🕐 **Closed mid-Jan–mid-Feb**

Clifden
Co Galway
Rock Glen (££)
Traditional hospitality and fine cuisine are provided in this beautifully converted 18th-century shooting lodge.

☎ 095-21035 & 21393
🕐 **Closed Nov–mid-Mar**

Doolin
Co Clare
Aran View House (££)
This attractive and comfortable hotel is set in farmland, with panoramic views of the Aran Islands.

✉ **Coast Road** ☎ 065-74061 & 74420

Ennistymon
Co Clare
Grovemount House (£)
A smart, purpose-built guesthouse on high ground on the edge of the town, convenient for both The Burren and the Clare coast.

✉ **Lahinch Road**
☎ 065-71431 & 71038
🕐 **Closed Nov–Mar**

Galway
Co Galway
Glenlo Abbey (£££)
A restored 18th-century abbey offering first-class accommodation and fine food. The hotel is set in a landscaped estate overlooking the lough.

✉ **Bushypark** ☎ 091-526666

Killeen House (£)
An award-winning guesthouse, beautifully appointed and decorated, in 10ha of grounds that stretch down to the shores of the lough.

✉ **Killeen, Bushypark** ☎ 091 524179 🕐 **Closed 23–8 Dec**

Knockferry
Co Galway
Knockferry Lodge (£)
On the shores of Lough Corrib, this farmhouse offers cosy accommodation and a warm welcome.

☎ 091-80122 🕐 **Closed Oct–Apr**

Roundstone
Co Galway
Eldon's (££)
A distinctive blue-and-yellow painted building in this picturesque fishing village, Eldon's has a popular restaurant which specialises in local seafood.

✉ **Main Street** ☎ 095-35933 & 35942 🕐 **Closed 20 Dec–17 Mar**

The North

Annalong
Co Down
Glassdrumman Lodge (£££)
Warm hospitality and simple excellence are the hallmarks of this tremendous hotel.
✉ 85 Mill Road ☎ 013967-68451

Belfast
Culloden (£££)
One of Northern Ireland's foremost hotels, in a mansion overlooking Belfast Lough.
✉ Bangor Road, Holywood ☎ 01232-425223 ⏰ Closed 24–5 Dec

Bushmills
Co Antrim
White Gables (£)
This impeccable modern guesthouse is on the coast road and has good views.
✉ 83 Dunluce Road ☎ 01265-731611

Coleraine
Co Londonderry
Greenhill House (£)
A lovely Georgian country house with immaculate, well equipped bedrooms.
✉ 24 Greenhill Road, Aghadowey ☎ 01265-868241 ⏰ Closed Dec–Feb

Donegal
Co Donegal
Harvey's Point (££)
On Lough Eske's shore, this modern hotel has spacious bedrooms and excellent cuisine.
✉ Lough Eske, on N56 ☎ 073-22208 ⏰ Closed weekdays Nov–Mar

Dungannon
Co Tyrone
Grange Lodge (£)
A first class guesthouse set in 8ha of gardens. Bedrooms are individually styled and home cooking is served.
✉ 7 Grange Road ☎ 01868-784212 ⏰ Closed 21 Dec–9 Jan

Lisburn
Co Antrim
Brook Lodge (£)
Comfortable accommodation and good farmhouse food in a modern bungalow.
✉ 79 Old Ballynahinch Road, Cargacroy ☎ 01846-638454

Maghera
Co Londonderry
Ardtara Country House (££)
A charming 19th-century country house offering high quality accommodation.
✉ 8 Gorteade Road (phone for directions) ☎ 01648-44490

Portaferry
Co Down
Portaferry Hotel (££)
Charming hotel overlooking the lough, serving good wholesome food.
✉ 10 The Strand ☎ 012477-28231 ⏰ Lunch, dinner. Closed 24–5 Dec. Opposite Strangford Lough ferry terminal

Portrush
Co Antrim
Ramore Restaurant (£££)
A popular waterside restaurant with uncomplicated cooking. The emphasis is on seafood.
✉ The Harbour ☎ 01265-824313 ⏰ Lunch, dinner. Closed 24–6 Dec

Rossnowlagh
Co Donegal
Sand House (££)
On a crescent of golden sands with sea views, this hotel is well known for its hospitality, cuisine and service.
☎ 072-51777 ⏰ Closed mid-Oct–Easter

Europa Hotel
Most hotels strive for recognition and are only too pleased to be described with superlatives, but Belfast's Europa Hotel cannot have been too delighted with its fame – as 'the most bombed hotel'. On the bright side, this has resulted in splendid refurbishment, so that the Europa is now a truly international hotel with excellent facilities.

✉ Great Victoria Street
☎ 01232-327000
⏰ Closed 24–5 Dec (£££)

Department Stores, Crafts & Music Shops

Quality Crafts
The Irish pride in fine craftsmanship is reflected in the number of visitor attractions that offer quality crafts in their gift shops. Right alongside the souvenir key rings and packets of shamrock seed you will find glittering crystal, fine pottery, linen, Celtic jewellery and beautiful tweeds and woollens. The same is true of the major Tourist Information Centres, which offer a splendid showcase for Irish goods.

Department Stores

East
W H Good
✉ 88–90 High Street, Kilkenny, Co Kilkenny ☎ 056-22143

Hores
✉ 31 South Main Street, Wexford, Co Wexford
☎ 053-42200

Winston's
✉ 105 Main Street, Bray, Co Dublin ☎ 01-2869011

Winston's
✉ Parliament Street, Kilkenny, Co Kilkenny ☎ 056-21699

South
Cash & Co
✉ Patrick Street, Cork, Co Cork
☎ 021-276771

Merricks of Youghal
✉ 80–82 North Main Street, Youghal, Co Cork
☎ 024-92737

Todds
✉ 16 O'Connell Street, Limerick, Co Limerick
☎ 061-417222

West
Thos Burgess
✉ 1 Church Street, Athlone, Co Westmeath
☎ 0902-72005

Moons
✉ Eglinton buildings, Galway, Co Galway ☎ 091-565254

T Naughton
✉ 35/6 Shop Street, Galway, Co Galway ☎ 091-563061

Roches
✉ Corrib Shopping Centre, Eyre Street, Galway, Co Galway
☎ 091-561211

Anthony Ryan
✉ 16–18 Shop Street, Galway, Co Galway ☎ 091-567061

North
Austin & Co
✉ 2 The Diamond, Londonderry, Co Londonderry
☎ 01504-261817

House of Brindle
✉ 20 Windsor Avenue, Lurgan, Co Armagh
☎ 01762-321721

A Lennox & Sons
✉ 17/19 Market Street, Armagh, Co Armagh ☎ 01861-522288

T K Maxx
✉ Castle Court, Royal Avenue, Belfast ☎ 01232-331151

Moores of Coleraine
✉ 7–11 Church Street, Coleraine, Co Londonderry
☎ 01265-44444

White House
✉ 45 Main Street, Portrush, Co Antrim ☎ 01265-822244

Crafts

East
Avoca Handloom Weavers
Attractive woolens, knits and even china.
✉ Millmount Mills, Avoca, Co Wicklow ☎ 0402-35105

Blarney Woollen Mills
Large shop selling Irish tweed, knitwear, clothing, christening robes.
✉ 21–23 Nassau Street, Dublin
☎ 01-6710068

Design Ireland Plus
Irish-made clothes, pottery, glass and leather.
✉ 49 Fleet Street, Dublin
☎ 01- 6791322

Dublin Crystal
Full range of crystal; visitors can watch it being made on the premises.
✉ **Brookfield Terrace, off Carysfort Avenue, Blackrock, Co Dublin** ☎ 01-2887932

Dublin Woollen Mills
Old, established retail outlet for Irish knitwear.
✉ **41 Lower Ormond Quay, Dublin** ☎ 01-6775014

Kilkenny Design Centre
Extensive range of Irish crafts, clothing, linen, ceramics.
✉ **Castleyard, Kilkenny, Co Kilkenny** ☎ 056-22118

The Kilkenny Shop
Large store with a wide range of Irish crafts and clothing
✉ **Nassau Street, Dublin** ☎ 01-6777066

The Meetings Craft Shop
Craftshop and pub close to the location for the filming of the popular TV series, *Ballykissangel.*
✉ **Meeting of the Waters, Vale of Avoca, Avoca, Co Wicklow** ☎ 0402-35226

The Sweater Shop
A good selection of Irish knitwear.
✉ **9 Wicklow Street, Dublin** ☎ 01-6713270

The Sweater Shop
A good selection of Irish knitwear.
✉ **81 High Street, Kilkenny, Co Kilkenny** ☎ 056-63405

South
Throughout this region there are a large number of craft shops, galleries and workshops where crafts-people can be seen at work, including potters, weavers and artists, particularly in Killarney, Courtmacsherry and Shanagarry.

Aisling Crafts and Sweaters
Irish knitwear and rcrafts.
✉ **11 Oliver Plunkett Street, Cork, Co Cork** ☎ 021-276738

Black Abbey Crafts
Pottery, clothing, jewellery.
✉ **28 Main Street, Kenmare, Co Kerry** ☎ 064-42115

Blarney Woollen Mills
Large shop selling Irish tweed, knitwear, clothing.
✉ **Blarney, Co Cork** ☎ 021-385280

Boland Kinsale Crafts
Irish glass, linen and jewellery.
✉ **Barrys Place, Kinsale, Co Cork** ☎ 021-772161

Carrigdhoun Pottery
Tableware and souvenirs.
✉ **Main Street, Carrigaline, Co Cork** ☎ 021-372305

Celtic Crafts
Traditional craftware.
✉ **The Tracks, Dingle, Co Kerry** ☎ 066-52166

Crafts Centre
Local crafts, especially copper.
✉ **Blennerville, Co Kerry** ☎ 066-24233

Crafts of Ireland
Quality handmade Irish pottery, jewellery and weaving.
✉ **11 Winthrop Street, Cork, Co Cork** ☎ 021-275864

Designs
Pottery, knitwear, glass and furniture.
✉ **32 Main Street, Skibbereen, Co Cork** ☎ 028-21221

Gap of Dunloe Industries
The Avoca Handloom Weavers shop here has a selection of woven woollens and other craft items.
✉ **Gap of Dunloe, Co Kerry** ☎ 064-44144

Kilkenny Workshops
Frequently, while driving through rural Ireland, you will see signs for craft workshops, but the county of Kilkenny is particularly well endowed with them. The Kilkenny Design Workshops began the resurgence of high quality Irish crafts in the 1960s, and their example attracted many talented artists and craft workers to the area.

Undercover Market
The English Market, off Patrick Street, is one of Cork's old institutions and is great fun to stroll through. It is a huge undercover market packed with stalls, mostly selling foodstuffs of a traditional Irish nature, though a few more exotic items have begun to appear.

Irish Arts and Crafts
Jewellery, pottery, prints and music. Sporting tours arranged.
✉ 8 Main Street, Kinsale, Co Cork ☎ 021-774355

Mary Barry Weaving
Richly coloured woollen ladies' jackets, scarves and hats.
✉ 70 North Main Street, Cork, Co Cork ☎ 021-277302

Waterford Crystal
World famous crystal; factory tours are also available.
✉ N25 Cork road, Waterford ☎ 051-73311

West
Archway Craft Centre
A small shop which specialises in unusual knitwear and glass.
✉ Victoria Place, Eyre Square, Galway, Co Galway ☎ 091-563693

Avoca Handweavers
High quality Irish tweed and knitwear. The shop also has a coffee room;
✉ Dooneen Haven, Letterfrack, Co Galway ☎ 095-41058

Connemara Marble Industries
A selection of items, carved from the locally quarried green marble.
✉ Moycullen, Co Galway, on the main Galway–Clifden road, 13km west of Galway, ☎ 559-85102, 85746 & 23079

Connemara Pottery Studio
Pottery made on the premises.
✉ Ardbear, Clifden, Co Galway ☎ 095-21254

Connemara Woollen Mills Craft Shop
Wide range of woollens and clothing.
✉ Westport Road, Clifden, Co Galway ☎ 095-21122

Design Ireland Plus
Pottery, glass, leather and ties.
✉ The Cornstore, Middle Street, Galway, Co Galway ☎ 091-567716

Design Ireland Plus
Pottery, glass, leather and ties.
✉ Lower Abbeygate Street, Galway, Co Galway ☎ 091-566620

Foxford Woollen Mills
Famous mill with historical tours; blankets, rugs, tweeds.
✉ Foxford, Co Mayo ☎ 094-56756

Galway Irish Crystal Heritage Centre
Workshop tours, displays and fine crystal.
✉ Merlin Park, Dublin Road, Galway, Co Galway ☎ 091-757311

Round Tower Crafts and Gift Shop
Wide range of Irish crafts.
✉ Church Street, Killala, Co Mayo ☎ 096-32769

North
Belleek Pottery Visitor Centre
Guided tours, audio-visual theatre, museum and showroom.
✉ Belleek, Co Fermanagh ☎ 013656-58501

The Craft Centre The Craft Village
Multitude of local designs under one roof.
✉ 25 The Village Shipquay Street, Londonderry, Co Londonderry ☎ 01504-261876

Craftworks Gallery
Showcase for local pieces.
✉ 13 Linenhall Street, Belfast ☎ 01232-236334

Craftworks Shop
Wide variety of local and Irish crafts.

✉ **Bedford House, Bedford Street, Belfast** ☎ 01232-244465

Crane Gallery
Handcrafted jewellery, pottery and clocks.
✉ **15 Broughshane Street, Ballymena, Co Antrim**
☎ 01266-40569

Enniskillen Craft and Design Centre
Centre for a number of craft-workers to produce and sell. their work
✉ **The Buttermarket, Enniskillen, Co Fermanagh**
☎ 01365-324499

Ferguson Linen Centre
All types of Irish linen. Two factory tours daily.
✉ **54 Scarva Road, Banbridge, Co Down** ☎ 018206-23491

Fermanagh Cottage Industries
Contemporary crafts and ceramics; Celtic-style jewellery.
✉ **14 East Bridge Street, Enniskillen, Co Fermanagh**
☎ 01365-322260

Fermanagh Crystal
Crystal is made and sold on the premises. Workshop viewing.
✉ **Main Street, Co Fermanagh**
☎ 013656-58631

Irish Linen Stores
Linen from all over Ireland.
✉ **Fountain Centre, College Street, Belfast** ☎ 01232-322727

The Irish Shop
A good range of traditional jewellery and Irish linen.
✉ **2 Waterloo Street, Londonderry, Co Londonderry**
☎ 01504-271149

Ulster Weavers
Irish linen goods, including kitchenware and gifts. Visitors can tour the factory and see the weavers at work.
✉ **44 Montgomery Road, Belfast** ☎ 01232-404236

Traditional Music Tapes & CDs

East
Celtic Note
A–Z of Irish artists, classical and instrumental including Breton and Scottish Celtic.
✉ **Nassau Street, Dublin**
☎ 01-6704157

Claddagh Records
Irish traditional and folk music specialists.
✉ **2 Cecilia Street, Temple Bar, Dublin** ☎ 01-6770262

Musicians Inc
Guitar specialist. Also sells mandolins and Celtic drums.
✉ **56 Lower George's Street, Dun Laoghaire, Co Dublin**
☎ 01-2300626

The Payback
Mainly Indie.
✉ **17 Temple Bar, Dublin**
☎ 01-6799097

Record Collector Basement
Buy/sell/exchange, also music books and videos.
✉ **30 Wicklow Street, Dublin**
☎ 01-6791909

South
Kelly's
Acoustic instruments, tapes and books.
✉ **15 Grand Parade, Cork, Co Cork** ☎ 021-272355

West
Roundstone Musical Instruments
Make and sell hand-held Celtic drums, many with individual artwork. Visitors can see these being made.
✉ **IDA Craft Centre, Roundstone, Co Galway**
☎ 095-35875

Traditional Music Shop
CD's, tapes and vinyl, in one of Ireland's main centres of traditional music.
✉ **Fisher Street, Doolin, Co Clare** ☎ 065-74407

Modern Shopping
The Square Towncentre at Tallaght, just south of Dublin, is a superb modern shopping centre, the largest in Ireland, with nearly 150 shops under a huge dome of natural light. Trees and shrubs thrive in these conditions, creating an illusion of the outdoors where it never rains. The centre, open every day, also includes a 12-screen cinema, restaurants, a free crèche and free parking for 3,000 cars.

Antiques

Linen Goods

Irish linen is known all over the world, but the industry suffered enormously with the advent of new, cheaper fibres. Though it is unlikely that it will ever achieve the heights of its 19th-century heyday, the linen industry is enjoying a renewed interest, and fine quality goods are still being produced in Northern Ireland.

East

Conlon Antiques
Architectural and shop fittings.
✉ **21 Lower Clanbrassil Street, Dublin** ☎ **01-4537323**

Ha'penny Bridge Galleries
Decorative furniture.
✉ **15 Bachelors Walk, Dublin** ☎ **01-8723950**

Mother Redcap's Indoor Market
Open Fri, Sat and Sun.
✉ **Back Lane, Dublin** ☎ **01 4540656**

O'Neill's Treasure Trove
Old Belleek pottery.
✉ **Carrigarnon, on main Dublin–Belfast road, Dundalk, Co Louth** ☎ **042-71222**

Phelan Antiques
Furniture; do own restoration.
✉ **Ballybought Street, Kilkenny, Co Kilkenny** ☎ **056-62338**

Whyte's
Stamps, coins and medals.
✉ **30 Marlborough Street, Dublin** ☎ **01-8746161**

South

Antiques & Curios
Victorian and Georgian specialist.
✉ **26 Rock Street, Tralee, Co Kerry** ☎ **066-23577**

Antiques & Curios Centre
Victorian and Georgian furniture and curios.
✉ **North Gate Bridge, Cork, Co Cork** ☎ **021-395320**

J F Burke
Edwardian furniture and soft furnishings.
✉ **The Square, Cahir, Co Tipperary** ☎ **052-41201**

Bygones Antiques
Pine country furniture and iron beds.
✉ **16 Nicholas Street, Limerick, Co Limerick** ☎ **061-417339**

A Fleury
Wide range of 18th- and 19th-century pieces.
✉ **The Square, Cahir, Co Tipperary** ☎ **052-41226**

Granny's Bottom Drawer
Traditionally made Irish linens.
✉ **53 Main Street, Kinsale, Co Cork** ☎ **021-774839**

Inné
Jewellery, Victorian period onwards.
✉ **11 Plunkett Street, Cork, Co Cork** ☎ **064-36200**

The Pinnacle
Georgian and Victorian pine.
✉ **McCurtain Street, Cork, Co Cork** ☎ **021-501319**

West

Arcadia Antiques
Jewellery and fine art.
✉ **Prince of Wales Hotel, Athlone, Co Westmeath** ☎ **0902-74671**

Arcadia Antiques
Jewellery, gifts, fine arts.
✉ **Castle Street, Galway, Co Galway** ☎ **091-561861**

Bygones of Ireland
Huge shop selling pine and country furniture.
✉ **Lodge Road, Westport, Co Mayo** ☎ **098-26132 & 25701**

Claddagh Antiques
Fine clocks, furniture, jewellery.

 Forster Court, Forster Street, Galway, Co Galway ☎ 091-563898

Clarenbridge Antiques
Irish Country farmhouse wares.
 Clarenbridge, Co Galway
☎ 091-796522

Cobwebs
Mainly Victorian jewellery.
 7 Quay Lane, Spanish Arch, Galway, Co Galway ☎ 091-564388

Doherty
Edwardian and Victorian specialist.
 Teeling Street, Sligo, Co Sligo ☎ 071 69494

Georgian Antiques
General antiques and jewellery.
 Johnston Court, Sligo, Co Sligo ☎ 071-62421

Honan's Antiques
Victorian pine country furniture.
 Crowe Street, Gort, Co Galway ☎ 091-631407

Maguires Antiques of Galway
Victorian and Edwardian furniture and art.
 Kiltartan House, Forster Street, Galway, Co Galway
☎ 091-566698

Sligo Antiques
Good general selection.
 O'Connell Street, Sligo, Co Sligo ☎ 071-46477

Tony Honan
Clocks, oil lamps, Irish china, and general small items.
 Abbey Street, Ennis, Co Clare ☎ 065-28137

Twice as Nice
Classic and vintage clothes and textiles. Also antique gold, silver and lace.
 5 Quay Street, Spanish Arch, Galway, Co Galway ☎ 091-566332

North

Antiques by Patrick Bradley
Oriental rugs specialist.
 2 London Street, Londonderry, Co Londonderry
☎ 01504-377811

Archway Antiques
A courtyard complex of nine antique shops and three art galleries.
 Hoops Courtyard, 7 Main Street, Greyabbey, Co Down
☎ 012477-88889

Ballinderry Antiques
Edwardian and Victorian antiques and silver.
 Upper Ballinderry (on A26), Lisburn, Co Antrim ☎ 01846-651046

Balmoral Antiques
Victorian fire screens, tables, jugs and pots.
 661 Lisburn Road, Belfast
☎ 01232-665221

Carroll's Antiques
Georgian, Victorian and Edwardian items.
 82 Donegall Pass, Belfast
☎ 01232-238246

Castledawson Mill
A huge antique centre in a converted mill building, selling everything.
 Castledawson Mill, Moyola Road, Castledawson, Co Londonderry ☎ 01648-469353 & 01960-323817

Dunluce Antiques and Crafts
Restored porcelain and Irish art.
 33 Ballytober Road, Bushmills, Co Antrim
☎ 012657-31140

Terrace Antiques
Jewellery, porcelain, linen, small pieces of furniture and art deco items.
 441a Lisburn Road, Belfast
☎ 01232-663943

Mill Visits
The best way to visit the working mills is on the Irish Linen tour, a six-hour trip which includes lunch and the services of a knowledgeable guide. Tours leave Banbridge Gateway Tourist Information Centre on Wednesdays and Saturdays between May and September.

Animals, Aquaria, Parks & Trains

Riding
Children and ponies are always a good combination, and both hold a special interest in the hearts of the Irish. There are riding stables all over Ireland, and many of them organise trekking or trail riding through beautiful countryside. Tuition, hacking and cross-country courses are also widely available, and if your family is really enthusiastic, there are lots of equestrian holidays on offer. The Irish Tourist Board have full information.

East

Monkstown Co Dublin
Lambert Puppet Theatre and Museum
The only purpose-built puppet theatre in Ireland. Saturday matinée performances.
✉ Clifton Lane, Monkstown ☎ 01-2800974 🕐 all year daily. 🍴 Refreshments (£) 🚌 7, 7A or 8 bus from town centre 🚻 Good 🎭 Moderate

Dublin Zoo
An ideal family day out.
✉ Phoenix Park ☎ 01-6771425 🕐 Summer: Mon–Sat 9:30–5, Sun 10:30–6. Winter Mon–Fri & 9:30–4, Sat 9:30–5, Sun 10:30–5. 🍴 Restaurant, Cafés, Kiosks (£) 🚌 No 10 bus from O'Connell Street, Nos 25 & 26 from Middle Abbey Street 🚻 Good 🎭 Moderate

South

Ballyporeen, Co Tipperary
Mitchelstown Caves
The caves are renowned for their depth of 1km, and comprise two groups, Desmond's Cave and New Cave. Electric lighting casts mysterious shadows.
✉ ✉ Off the N8 4 km north of Ballyporeen ☎ 052-67246 🕐 all year 10–6 🚌 Buses from Dublin to Cork pass through Mitchelstown 🎭 Moderate

Fenit, Co Kerry
Fenit Seaworld
A voyage of undersea exploration.
✉ ThePier ☎ 066-36544 🕐 daily 10–5:30. Closed 24–5 Dec. 🍴 Refreshments (£) 🚌 No public transport 🚻 Good 🎭 Moderate

Fota, Co Cork
Fota Wildlife Park
Established by the Royal Zoological Society of Ireland, Fota Wildlife Park's primary aim is the breeding of endangered species. It is an open park – except for the cheetah!
✉ 1.5 km south of Cork Harbour ☎ 021-812678 🕐 Apr–Oct daily 🚌 No public transport 🚻 Few 🎭 Moderate

Tralee, Co Kerry
Tralee & Dingle Light Railway
Train rides to Blennerville Windmill, during the season. An on-board commentary is provided.
☎ 066-28888 🕐 Apr–Sep daily 11–5. Closed 2nd Mon & Tue of month 🚂 Trains on the hour from Tralee, on the half hour from Blennerville 🚻 Few 🎭 Moderate

West

Galway
Peter Pan Funworld
Children's amusement centre that's open conveniently long hours.
✉ Unit 4, Corbett Commercial Centre, Wellpark, Monivea Road, off the Dublin Road and the N6 at Moneenageisha Cross. ☎ 091-756505 🕐 All year daily 10–7 🚌 Bus from Galway 🚻 Few 🎭 Moderate

Lahinch, Co Clare
Seaworld
Leisure centre, incorporating an aquarium and swimming pool.
✉ The Promenade ☎ 065-81900 🕐 all year daily (telephone for details). 🍴 Refreshments (£) 🚌 Bus from Dublin 🚻 Good 🎭 Moderate

Letterfrack, Co Galway

Ocean's Alive

Local marine life with fish tanks, rock pools, touch pool and cruises.

✉ Off the N59 between Letterfrack and Renvyle.
☎ 095-43473 🕐 all year daily. May–Sep: 9:30–7; Oct–Apr: 10–4:30 🍽 Tea room (£) 🚌 No public transport 🚻 Good 👫 Moderate

Shannonbridge

Clonmacnoise & West Offaly Railway

Narrow-gauge railway tour of the Blackwater bog (9km) with on-board commentary.

☎ Bord na Muge railway tour ☎ 0905-74172 & 74114
🕐 Apr–Oct daily 10–5, trains leave on the hour 🍽 Coffee shop (£) 🚌 No public transport 🚻 Few 👫 Moderate

North

Ballycastle, Co Antrim

Watertop Farm

Sheep shearing, ornamental birds, tours.

✉ 188 Cushendall Road
☎ 012657-62576 🕐 Jul & Aug daily 10:30–5:30; weekends June & Sep 🍽 Tea room (£) 🚌 Ulsterbus from Ballycastle 🚻 Few 👫 Moderate

Ballymoney, Co Antrim

Leslie Hill Heritage Farm Park

Working farm with horse and trap rides, rare breeds, nature trails, lake, museum.

✉ Macfin Road ☎ 012656-66803 🕐 Easter–May: Sun & bank hols 2–6. Jun: Sat & Sun 2–6. Jul–Aug: Mon–Sat 11–6, Sun 2–6. Sep: Sun 2–6 🍽 Tea room (£) 🚌 No public transport 🚻 Few 👫 Moderate

Belfast

Belfast Zoo

A wide range of animals are housed in enclosures

designed in the 1980s.

✉ Antrim Road ☎ 01232-776277 🕐 daily 10–3:30 (2:30 Fri). Closed 25 Dec
🍽 Refreshments (£) 🚌 Nos 45 & 49 buses from City Hall
🚻 Good 👫 Moderate

Balleymoney, Co Antrim

Causeway Safari Park

Lions and other exotic wildlife. Mini zoo.

✉ 28 Benvarden Road, Derry Keighan ☎ 012657-41067
🕐 Apr, May & Sep, Sat & Sun only 10:30–6:30. Jun–Aug: daily 10:30–6:30 🍽 Refreshments (£)
🚌 No 171 bus from Coleraine 👫 Moderate

Creggan, Co Tyrone

An Creagán Visitor Centre

Adventure play area, bicycles for hire, walking and cyling.

☎ 016627-61112 🕐 all year. Apr–Sep: daily 11–6:30. Oct–Mar: Mon–Fri 11–4:30
🍽 Licensed restaurant (££)
🚌 No public transport 🚻 Few 👫 Cheap

Downpatrick

Downpatrick Steam Railway

A 1.5km section of the old branch line to Ardglass has been restored. There are also displays in the station buildings.

✉ Market Street ☎ 01396-615779 & 617517 🕐 station house Mon–Fri 9–5, Sat 10–4; train rides Easter Sun & Mon, Sun Jul–mid-Sep, plus Hallowe'en and Christmas specials 🍽 Refreshments (£)
👫 Moderate

Portaferry, Co Down

Exploris

One of Europe's finest aquaria with huge Open Sea Tank with side views, touch tanks, and so on.

✉ The Rope Walk ☎ 012477-28062 🕐 all year. Mon–Fri 10–5, Sat 11–5, Sun 1–5 🍽 Tea room (£) 🚌 No public transport 🚻 Good 👫 Moderate

Story-telling

'Tell me a story' is a request that would hardly ever go unheeded in Ireland – often you don't even need to ask – and story-telling is a tradition that goes back far beyond the written word. Ancient myths and legends have been perpetuated in many forms and new stories added. The art of story-telling is still alive in parts of the West and South, and all ages are enthralled. Three notable story-telling festivals are the Sean McCarthy Memorial Week in Listowel, Co Kerry, in August, one on Cape Clear, Co Cork, in September and the North-West Story-telling Festival at Londonderry in March.

Theatres, Concert Halls & Banquets

Buskers
Dublin's Grafton Street is famous as much for its buskers as for its excellent shopping. The variety of open-air acts is enormous, and in strolling the length of the street you might hear such diverse sounds as a lone penny whistle playing traditional jigs and reels, a classical string quartet, a South American band and a jazz or rock guitarist. The quality varies too, but all are hugely entertaining and contribute to the Street's unique atmosphere.

Theatres

East

Abbey
✉ Abbey Street, Dublin ☎ 01-8787222

Andrews Lane Theatre
✉ 9 St Andrews Lane, Dublin ☎ 01-6795720

Backstage Theatre & Centre for the Arts
✉ Farneyhoogan, Co Longford ☎ 043-47889

Corn Mill Theatre & Arts Centre
✉ Carrigallen, Co Leitrim ☎ 049-39612

Dublin Youth Theatre
✉ 23 Upper Gardiner Street, Dublin ☎ 01-8743687

Duchas Folk Theatre
✉ Castle Street, Trim, Co Meath ☎ 046-36342

Gaiety
✉ South King Street, Dublin ☎ 01-6771717

Garage Theatre
✉ Monaghan, ☎ 047-81597

Gate
✉ 1 Cavendish Row, Dublin ☎ 01-8744045

Grove Theatre
✉ Leinster Street, Athy, Co Kildare ☎ 0507-38375

Olympia
✉ Dame Street, Dublin ☎ 01-677744

Peacock
☎ 01-8787222

The Point
✉ National Exhibition Centre, Dublin ☎ 01-8366777

Project Arts Centre
✉ 39 East Essex Street, Dublin ☎ 01-6712321

Riverbank Studio/Theatre
✉ 10 Merchants Quay, Dublin ☎ 01-6773370

St Anthony's Theatres
✉ Merchants Quay, Dublin ☎ 01-6777651

St Michael's Theatre
✉ New Ross, Co Wexford ☎ 051-421255

Theatre Royal
✉ High Street, Wexford, Co Wexford ☎ 053-22400

Watergate Theatre
✉ Parliament Street, Kilkenny, Co Kilkenny ☎ 056-61674

South

Belltable Arts Centre
✉ 69 O'Connell Street, Limerick, Co Limerick ☎ 061-319866

Cork Arts and Theatre Club
✉ 7 Knapps Square, Cork, Co Cork ☎ 021-508398

Craic Na Coillte Teo
✉ Scartagh, Clonakilty, Co Cork ☎ 023-34555

Everyman Palace Theatre
✉ McCurtain Street, Cork ☎ 021-501673

Exiles
✉ 77 Grand Parade, Cork ☎ 021-278415

Firkin Crane Cultural Centre
✉ Shandon ☎ 021-507487

The Forum
✉ The Glen, Waterford, Co Cork ☎ 051-55038

Garter Lane Theatre
✉ 22A O'Connell Street, Waterford, Co Cork ☎ 061-877153

Phoenix Theatre
✉ Gas House Lane, Tipperary, Co Tipperary ☎ 062-33266

Regal Theatre
✉ Davis Road, Clonmel, Co Tipperary ☎ 052-21689

St Michael's Theatre
✉ South Street, New Ross, Co Wexford ☎ 051-874402

Schoolyard Theatre
✉ Main Street, Charleville, Co Cork ☎ 063-81844

Siamsa Tire Theatre, The National Theatre of Ireland
✉ Between Princess Street and the Ashe Memorial Hall, Tralee, Co Kerry ☎ 066-23055

Theatre Royal
✉ Upper Cecil Street, Limerick, Co Limerick ☎ 061-414224

Theatre Royal
✉ The Mall, Waterford, Co Cork ☎ 051-874402

Triskal Arts Centre
✉ Tobin Street, Cork ☎ 021-272022

White Memorial Theatre
✉ Wolfe Tone Street, Clonmel, Co Tipperary ☎ 052-23333

West
Druid Theatre
✉ Chapel Lane, Galway, Co Galway ☎ 091-568617

Folk Theatre (An Taibhdhearc)
✉ Middle Street, Galway, Co Galway ☎ 091-755479

Hawk's Well Theatre
✉ Johnston COurt, Sligo, Co Sligo ☎ 071-61526

Punchbag Theatre
✉ 6 Quay Lane, Spanish Arch, Galway, Co Galway ☎ 091-565422

St Brigid's Theatre
✉ Town Hall, Glenamaddy, Co Galway ☎ 907-59570

Theatre Omnibus
✉ Francis Street, Ennis, Co Clare ☎ 065-29952

Town Hall Theatre
✉ Courthouse Square, Woodquay, Galway, Co Galway ☎ 091-569777

Travellers Friend
✉ Old Westport Road, Castlebar, Co Mayo ☎ 094-23111

The North
Ardhowen Theatre
✉ Dublin Road, Enniskillen, Co Fermanagh ☎ 01365-325440

Balor Theatre
✉ Main Street, Ballybofey, Co Donegal ☎ 074-31840

Belfast Civic Arts Theatre
✉ 23–41 Botanic Avenue, Belfast ☎ 01232-316900

Clotworthy House Arts Centre
✉ Randalstown Road, Antrim, Co Antrim ☎ 01849-428000

Courtyard Theatre
✉ 585 Doagh Road, Newtownabbey, Co Antrim ☎ 01232-848287

Dun Uladh, The Cultural Heritage Centre of Ulster
✉ Ballnamullan, Omagh, Co Tyrone ☎ 01662-242777

Festivals
The number and variety of Irish festivals – both internationally important and small local events – is enormous. Music festivals include classical, opera, jazz, country and western and traditional Irish music and dancing, sometimes with competitions for pipers and bodhrán players. Arts festivals encompass drama, poetry readings and literary competitions. There are sporting festivals, including horse-racing, golf, sailing and angling; there are also gourmet festivals, film festivals and flower festivals. Many take place in the summer, but visitors will find something going on somewhere in every month of the year.

Music Sessions

Traditional music sessions are widespread throughout Ireland, but the west has a particularly rich heritage. Some city pubs will have a session every night, with different musicians at each, and even in the country there will be a session somewhere within easy reach. Sessions are informal and unrehearsed, but the fiddlers, flautists, whistlers, pipers, bodrhán players and whoever else may turn up all know the tunes and standards are usually very high.

Foyle Arts Centre
✉ Lawrence Hill, Londonderry, Co Londonderry ☎ 01504-360196 & 365419

Grand Opera House
✉ Great Victoria Street, Belfast ☎ 01232-241919

Group Theatre
✉ Bedford Street, Belfast ☎ 01232-329685

Lyric Theatre
✉ 55 Ridgeway Street, Belfast ☎ 01232-381081, 669463 & 669660

Old Museum Arts Centre
✉ 7 College Square North, Belfast ☎ 01232-235053 & 233332

Playhouse
✉ St Colum's Hall, Artillery Street, Londonderry, Co Londonderry
☎ 01504-264481

Rialto Entertainments Centre
✉ Marlet Street. Londonderry, Co Londonderry ☎ 01504-262567

Riverside Theatre
✉ Cromore Road, Coleraine, Co Londonderry
☎ 01265-51388

St Columb's Theatre and Arts Centre
✉ Orchard Street, Londonderry, Co Londonderry
☎ 01504-262880, 262845 & 267789

Ulster Hall
✉ Bedford Street, Belfast
☎ 01232-323900

Waterfront Hall
✉ 2 Lanyon Place, Belfast
☎ 01232-334455

Concert Halls

The East
Bank of Ireland Arts Centre
Classical recitals in the former Parliament building.
✉ Foster Place, Dublin ☎ 01-6776801

Culturiann nah Eireann
✉ Belgrave Square, Monkstown Co Dublin ☎ 01-2800295

Father Matthew Hall
✉ 133 Church Street, Dublin
☎ 01-8731701

National Concert Hall
✉ Earlsfort Terrace, Dublin
☎ 01-7611533

The Point
✉ National Exhibition Centre, North Wall Quay, Dublin ☎ 01-8366777

Project Arts Centre
✉ 39 East Essex Street, Temple Bar, Dublin ☎ 01-6712321

Seomra an Cheoil   The Music Room
✉ 43 East Essex Street, Temple Bar, Dublin ☎ 01-6717009

Temple Bar Music Centre
✉ Curved Street, Temple Bar, Dublin ☎ 01-6777349

South
Bru Boru Heritage Centre (Comhaltas Ceoltoiri Eireann)
✉ At the foot of the Rock of Cashel, Cashel, Co Tipperary
☎ 062-62041

The Concert Hall
✉ University of Limerick, Limerick, Co Limerick ☎ 061-331549

Duchas House Cultural Music Centre (Comhaltas Ceoltori Eireann)
✉ Edward Street, Tralee, Co Kerry ☎ 01662-4083

Opera House
✉ Lavitt's Quay, Cork, Co Cork ☎ 021-270022

Teach Cheoil
✉ Village centre, Glenstall Abbey, Co Limerick ☎ 061-386103

North

Belfast Waterfront Hall
✉ Cecil Ward Building, 6–10 Linen Hall Street, Belfast ☎ 01232-33440

Grand Opera House
✉ Great Victoria Street, Belfast ☎ 01232-241919

Harty Room
✉ Queens University, Belfast ☎ 01232-245133

Whitla Hall
✉ Queens University, University Road, Belfast ☎ 01232-245133

Banquets

East
Dublin's Viking Feast
✉ Essex Quay, Temple Bar, Dublin ☎ 01-6057777 & 6796040

South
Bunratty Castle
✉ Bunraty, Co Galway ☎ 061-360788 ⊙ All year

Killarney Manor
✉ Loretto Road, Killarney, Co Kerry ☎ 064-31551 ⊙ Five nights a week from Apr–Oct

Knappogue Castle
✉ Quin, Co Galway ☎ 061-360788 ⊙ May–Oct

West
The Aran Ceili Banquet
✉ Dun Aonghasa Seafood Restaurant, Kilronan, Aran Islands, Co Galway ☎ 099-61104 or Galway Tourist Office 091-563081

Cinemas

East
Omniplex
✉ The Bridge Centre, Tullamore, Co Offaly ☎ 0506-22800

UCI
✉ The Square Town Centre, Tallaght, Co Dublin ☎ 01-4598170

Virgin Multiplex
✉ Dublin ☎ 01-8728400

South
Capital Cineplex
✉ Grand Parade, Cork, Co Cork ☎ 021-272216

Cinedrome 32
✉ Upper Castle Street, Tralee, Co Kerry ☎ 066-21055

Savoy Cineplex
✉ Bedford Row, Limerick, Co Limerick ☎ 061-311900

West
Omniplex
✉ Headford Road, Galway, Co Galway ☎ 091-567800 & 566771

North
Cineplex
✉ 1 Fountain Hill, Antrim, Co Antrim ☎ 01861-461111

Cine World
✉ Kennedy Centre, Falls Road, Belfast ☎ 01232-600988

Strand Multiplex
✉ Quayside Centre, Strand ☎ 01504-373939 & 373900

Themed Events

A number of visitor attractions provide occasional entertainment, such as classical concerts in historic houses, living history events at museums. In the North, the Ulster American Folk Park near Omagh has established a popular annual Appalachian and Blue Grass Music Festival and Carrikfergus and Dundrum Castles have medieval fairs, with all kind of suitable entertainments and all participants in costume.

What's On When

Irish Celebrations

There are many festivals and events staged throughout Ireland ranging from horse-racing to story-telling. Almost all involve music of some sort, often traditional, and all will guarantee you a day of fun. Opposite is a month-by-month selection of some of the major events held in the Republic and Northern Ireland. For further information and precise dates, contact the local tourist office.

February

Arts Festival, Portadown, Co Armagh
Ulster Harp Lager National, Downpatrick Racecourse, Co Down

March

Dublin Film Festival
Belfast Music Festival
St Patrick's Day – various pilgrimages and parades
Northwest Storytelling Festival, Londonderry, Co Londonderry

April

Folk Festival, Killarney, Co Kerry
Irish Grand National, Fairyhouse Racecourse,
World Irish Dancing Championships, Limerick, Co Limerick
Pan Celtic Festival, Galway, Co Galway

May

Belfast Civic Festival and Lord Mayor's Show
Mallow Folk Festival, Co Cork
International Jazz and Blues Festival, Londonderry, Co Londonderry

June

The Clare Festival of Traditional Song, Ennistymon, Co Clare
Queen of the Sea Festival, Castletownbere, Co Cork
Belfast Proms, Ulster Hall
Belfast Folk Festival

July

Festival of the Erne, Belturbet, Co Cavan
International Folk Dance Festival, Cobh, Co Cork
Independence Day Celebrations, Ulster American Folk Park, Co Tyrone

International Music Festival, Coalisland, Co Tyrone
Rathlin Festival Week, Rathlin Island, Co Antrim

August

Ballyshannon International Folk Festival, Ballyshannon, Co Donegal.
Rose of Tralee Festival, Tralee, Co Kerry
Busking Festival, Ballybunion, Co Kerry
O'Carolan Harp and Traditional Music Festival, Keadue, Co Roscommon
Puck Fair, Killorglin, Co Kerry

September

Clarenbridge Oyster Festival, Clarenbridge, Co Galway
Galway International Oyster Festival, Co Galway.
Story Telling Festival, Cape Clear, Co Cork
Matchmaking Festival, Lisdoonvarna, Co Clare
Appalachian and Blue Grass Festival, Ulster American Folk Park, Omagh, Co Tyrone
Opera Northern Ireland, Belfast

October

Dublin Theatre Festival
Cork Jazz Festival
Cork Film Festival
Kinsale Gourmet Festival, Co Cork
Wexford Opera Festival, Wexford, Co Wexford.
Waterford International Festival of Light Opera, Waterford, Co Waterford

November

Belfast Festival at Queen's
Foyle Film Festival, Londonderry, Co Londonderry

December

Cinemagic Film Festival, Belfast

Practical Matters

The following abbreviations
have been used in this section:
NI   Northern Ireland
RI   Republic of Ireland

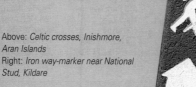

Above: *Celtic crosses, Inishmore,
Aran Islands*
Right: *Iron way-marker near National
Stud, Kildare*

TIME DIFFERENCES

GMT	Ireland	Germany	USA (NY)	Netherlands	Spain
12 noon	12 noon	1PM	7AM	1PM	1PM

BEFORE YOU GO

WHAT YOU NEED

●	Required					
○	Suggested					
▲	Not required	UK	Germany	USA	Netherlands	Spain
Passport/National Identity Card		▲	●	●	●	●
Visa		▲	▲	▲	▲	▲
Onward or Return Ticket		○	○	○	○	○
Health Inoculations		▲	▲	▲	▲	▲
Health Documentation (▶ 123, Health)		●	●	●	●	●
Travel Insurance		○	○	○	○	○
Driving Licence (national with English translation or International)		●	●	●	●	●
Car Insurance Certificate		●	●	●	●	●
Car Registration Document		●	●	●	●	●

WHEN TO GO

Dublin

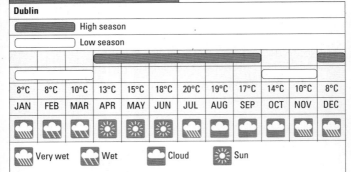

High season

Low season

8°C	8°C	10°C	13°C	15°C	18°C	20°C	19°C	17°C	14°C	10°C	8°C
JAN	FEB	MAR	APR	MAY	JUN	JUL	AUG	SEP	OCT	NOV	DEC

Very wet Wet Cloud Sun

TOURIST OFFICES

In the UK

Irish Tourist Board
150 New Bond
Street
London W1Y 0AQ
☎ 0171 493 3201
Fax: 0171 493 9065

Northern Ireland
Tourist Board
11 Berkeley Street
London W1X 5AD
☎ 0541 555250
Fax: 0171 409 0487

In the USA

Irish Tourist Board
345 Park Avenue
New York
NY 10154
☎ 212/418 0800
Fax: 212/371 9052

Northern Ireland
Tourist Board
551 Fifth Avenue
Suite 701, New York
NY 101766
☎ 212/922 0101
Fax: 212/922 0099

POLICE 999

FIRE 999

AMBULANCE 999

COASTAL RESCUE 999

WHEN YOU ARE THERE

ARRIVING

Scheduled flights operate from Britain, mainland Europe and North America to Dublin, Cork, Knock, Shannon and Belfast. The Republic's national airline is Aer Lingus (01-705 2222). Most ferry services from Britain arrive at Dun Laoghaire and Belfast.

Dublin Airport Kilometres to city centre	**Journey times**	
11 kilometres	🚊	N/A
	🚌	30 minutes
	🚗	20 minutes

Belfast Airport Kilometres to city centre	**Journey times**	
31 kilometres	🚊	60 minutes
	🚌	45 minutes
	🚗	45 minutes

MONEY

The monetary units are (in the Republic), the Irish punt, abbreviated as IR£, and (in Northern Ireland) the pound sterling (£). These are not interchangeable. On 1 January 1999 the euro became the official currency of the Republic of Ireland, and the Irish punt became a denomination of the euro. Irish punt notes and coins continue to be legal tender during a transitional period. Euro bank notes and coins are likely to start to be introduced by 1 January 2002.

Irish Punt (examples shown) are issued in 5, 10, 20, 50 notes and 1, 2, 5, 10, 20, 50 pence, IR£1 coins.

Pounds Sterling are issued in 5, 10, 20, 50 notes and 1, 2, 5, 10, 20, 50 pence, £1, £2 coins by the Bank of England, and in notes of 5, 10, 20, 50 (examples shown) by the provincial banks. Provincial bank notes are not accepted in other parts of the UK.

TIME

 Ireland observes Greenwich Mean Time (GMT), but from late March, when clocks are put forward one hour, until late October, summer time (GMT +1) operates.

CUSTOMS

➔ **YES**

Goods Obtained Duty Free Inside the EU or Goods Bought Outside the EU (Limits):
Alcohol (over 22° vol): 1L *or*
Alcohol (not over 22° vol): 2L *and* Still table wine: 2L
Cigarettes: 200 *or*
Cigars: 50 *or*
Tobacco: 250gms
Perfume: 60cc
Toilet water: 250cc

Goods Bought Duty and Tax Paid Inside the EU (Guidance Levels):
Alcohol (over 22° vol): 10L
Alcohol (not over 22° vol): 20L
Wine (max 60L sparkling): 90L
Beer: 110L
Cigarettes: 800 *or*
Cigars: 200 *or*
Tobacco: 1kg
Perfume: no limit
Toilet Water: no limit
You must be 17 and over to benefit from the alcohol and tobacco allowances.

 NO

Drugs, firearms, ammunition, offensive weapons, obscene material, unlicensed animals.

EMBASSIES

UK	Germany	USA	Netherlands	Spain
01-269 5211 (RI)	01265 44188 (NI)	01232 328239 (NI)	01574 261300 (NI)	01232 320148 (NI)
	01-269 3011 (RI)	01-668 8777 (RI)	01-269 3444 (RI)	01-283 8827 (RI)

WHEN YOU ARE THERE

TOURIST OFFICES

Republic of Ireland

- Dublin Tourism
  Suffolk Street
  Dublin 2
  ☎ 01-605 7797

- Southeast Tourism
  41 The Quay
  Waterford
  ☎ 051-875788

- Cork-Kerry Tourism
  Grand Parade
  Cork City
  ☎ 021-273251

- Shannon Development
  Tourism Division
  Shannon Town Centre
  Co Clare
  ☎ 061-361555

- Ireland West Tourism
  Victoria Place
  Eyre Square
  Galway City
  ☎ 091-563081

- Northwest Tourism
  Temple Street
  Sligo
  ☎ 071-61201

- Midlands East Tourism
  Clonard House
  Dublin Road
  Mullingar
  Co Westmeath
  ☎ 044-48650

Northern Ireland

- Tourist Information Centre
  St Anne's Court
  59 North Street
  Belfast BT1 1NB
  ☎ 01232 246609

NATIONAL HOLIDAYS

J	F	M	A	M	J	J	A	S	O	N	D
1		1(3)	(2)	2	1	1	2		1		2

1 Jan	New Year's Day
17 Mar	St Patrick's Day
Mar/Apr	Good Friday, Easter Monday
May (1st Mon)	May Holiday
May (last Mon)	Spring Holiday (NI)
Jun (1st Mon)	June Holiday (RI)
12 Jul	Orangeman's Day (NI)
Aug (1st Mon)	August Holiday (RI)
Aug (last Mon)	Late Summer Holiday (NI)
Oct (last Mon)	October Holiday (RI)
25 Dec	Christmas Day
26 Dec	St Stephen's Day

OPENING HOURS

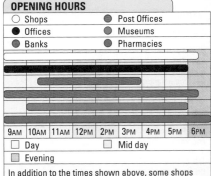

○ Shops   ● Post Offices
● Offices   ● Museums
● Banks   ● Pharmacies

9AM	10AM	11AM	12PM	2PM	3PM	4PM	5PM	6PM

☐ Day   ☐ Mid day
☐ Evening

In addition to the times shown above, some shops stay open till 8 or 9PM for late-night shopping on Thursday and Friday. Smaller towns and rural areas have an early closing day on one day a week. Nearly all banks are closed on Saturday and many post offices close at 1PM.

The opening times of museums and tourist sites vary and are subject to change; always check with a local tourist office. Many places close from October to March or have very limited opening, although most major sights are open all year.

DRIVE ON THE
LEFT

TOILETS
FREE

PUBLIC TRANSPORT

Internal Flights Flights from Dublin to other airports in Ireland are operated by Aer Lingus (☎ 01-705 2222) and Ryanair (☎ 01-844 4400). Aer Arann (☎ 091-593034) operates the Aran Flyer with several daily flights between the Aran Islands and Galway.

Trains In the Republic a limited network run by Iarnród Éireann (☎ 01-703 2358) serves major towns and cities. Trains are comfortable, generally reliable and fares reasonable. Northern Ireland Railways (☎ 01232 899411) operates services from Belfast to main towns and to Dublin.

Long Distance Buses In the Republic, Bus Éireann (☎ 01-836 6111) operates a network of express bus routes serving most of the country (some run summer only). In Northern Ireland, Ulsterbus (☎ 01232 333000), has links between Belfast and 23 towns. Unlimited travel tickets are available.

Ferries Two car ferries operate between Ballyhack, Co Wexford and Passage East, Co Waterford (☎ 051-82480) and Killimer, Co Clare and Tarbert, Co Kerry (☎ 065-53124), the latter saving 100km on the road journey. There are also ferry sevices from the mainland to some islands.

Urban Transport City bus services, particularly in Dublin and Belfast, are excellent. Dublin is served by Dublin Bus (☎ 01-873 4222) and also has a Rapid Transit system (DART). A 4-day ticket is available, covering bus and train travel, too. Citybus (☎ 01232 246485) serves the Belfast area.

CAR RENTAL

All of the international car rental firms are represented. A car from a local company, however, is likely to offer cheaper rates, but may not allow different pick-up/drop-off points. Car hire is also less expensive in Northern Ireland than the Republic.

TAXIS

Taxis are available in major towns and cities, at taxi stands or outside hotels, and at main rail stations, ports and airports. In Belfast, black cabs may be shared by customers and some operate rather like buses, shuttling their passengers between the city and the suburbs.

DRIVING

Speed limits on motorways and dual carriageways: **112kph**

Speed limits on country roads: **90kph**

Speed limits on urban roads: **48kph (or as signposted)**

Must be worn in front seats at all times and in rear seats where fitted.

Random breath-testing. Limit: 35 micrograms of alcohol in 100ml of breath

Leaded and unleaded petrol is widely available on both sides of the border. Fuel stations in villages in the Republic usually stay open till 8 or 9PM, and open after Mass on Sundays. In Northern Ireland, 24-hour fuel stations are fairly common. Fuel is cheaper in Northern Ireland than in the Republic.

If you break down driving your own car and are a member of an AIT-affiliated motoring club, you can call the Automobile Association's rescue service (☎ 1800 667788 in the Republic; ☎ 0990 500600 in Northern Ireland). If the car is hired follow the instructions given in the documentation; most of the international rental firms provide a rescue service.

PERSONAL SAFETY

The national police forces are:

RI – Garda Síochána (pronounced *sheekawnah*) in black-and-blue uniforms
NI – Royal Ulster Constabulary (RUC) in dark green uniforms.

- Be wary in suburban areas of Belfast, southern Co Armagh and Coalisland, Co Tyrone, which are prone to sectarian violence.
- Take care of personal property in Dublin.
- Avoid leaving property visible in cars.

Police assistance:
☎ **999**
from any call box

TELEPHONES

Public telephone boxes, blue and cream in the Republic and red in Northern Ireland, are being replaced by glass and metal booths. To make a call, lift the handset, insert the correct coins (10, 20 or 50 pence, or £1) or phonecard (available from post offices and newsagents), and dial.

International Dialling Codes

From Ireland to:	
UK:	**00 44** (RI only; no code needed from NI)
Germany:	**00 49**
USA:	**00 1**
Netherlands:	**00 31**
Spain:	**00 34**

POST

RI   NI

Post Offices
The main post offices in O'Connell Street, Dublin, and Castle Place, Belfast, are open extended hours, otherwise hours are:
Open: 9AM
Closed: 5:30PM (Sat: 1PM/RI, 12:30PM/NI)
☎ 01-705 7000 (RI)
☎ 01232 323740 (NI)

ELECTRICITY

The native power supply is: 230 volts (RI); 240 volts (NI)

Type of socket: 3 square-pin (UK type). Parts of the Republic also have 2 round-pin (continental type).
Overseas visitors should bring a good travel adaptor.

TIPS/GRATUITIES

Yes ✓ No ✗		
Restaurants (if service not included)	✓	10%
Cafés (if service not included)	✓	10%
Hotels (if service not included)	✓	10%
Hairdressers	✓	50p/£1
Taxis	✓	10%
Tour guides	✓	50p/£1
Cinema usherettes	✗	
Porters	✓	50p/bag
Cloakroom attendants	✓	50p
Toilets	✗	

Best times to photograph: early morning and late evening. Irish light can be dull so you may need faster film eg 200 or 400 ASA.

Where to buy film: film and camera batteries are readily available in many shops and pharmacies.

Restrictions: in Northern Ireland you cannot photograph inside museums or take photographs of military installations, vehicles or personnel.

HEALTH

Insurance
Nationals of EU and certain other countries can get medical treatment in Ireland with Form E111 (not required for UK nationals), although private medical insurance is still advised and is essential for all other visitors.

Dental Services
EU nationals or nationals of countries with which Ireland has a reciprocal agreement, can get dental treatment within the Irish health service with Form E111 (not needed for UK nationals). Others should take out private medical insurance.

Sun Advice
The sunniest months are May and June with on average 5–6½ hours of sun a day (the extreme southeast the sunniest), though July and August are the hottest. During these months you should take the normal precautions against the sun.

Drugs
Prescription and non-prescription drugs and medicines are available from pharmacies. When closed, most display on their doors the address of the nearest one open. In an emergency, contact the nearest hospital.

Safe Water
Tap water in Ireland is perfectly safe to drink. However, if you prefer to drink bottled water you will find it widely available.

CONCESSIONS

Students Holders of an International Student Identity Card can buy a Travelsave Stamp which entitles them to travel discounts including a 50 per cent reduction on Bus Éireann, Iarnród Éireann and Irish Ferries (between Britain and Ireland). Contact your local student travel agency for further details. The Travelsave Stamp can be purchased from USIT, 19 Aston Quay, O'Connell Bridge, Dublin 2 (☎ 01-677 8117).

Senior Citizens Many car hire companies give discounts to those over 50 or 55, as do some hotels and a few tourist attractions. Some tour companies offer special spring and autumn package deals.

CLOTHING SIZES

Ireland	UK	Rest of Europe	USA	
36	36	46	36	Suits
38	38	48	38	Suits
40	40	50	40	Suits
42	42	52	42	Suits
44	44	54	44	Suits
46	46	56	46	Suits
7	7	41	8	Shoes
7.5	7.5	42	8.5	Shoes
8.5	8.5	43	9.5	Shoes
9.5	9.5	44	10.5	Shoes
10.5	10.5	45	11.5	Shoes
11	11	46	12	Shoes
14.5	14.5	37	14.5	Shirts
15	15	38	15	Shirts
15.5	15.5	39/40	15.5	Shirts
16	16	41	16	Shirts
16.5	16.5	42	16.5	Shirts
17	17	43	17	Shirts
8	8	34	6	Dresses
10	10	36	8	Dresses
12	12	38	10	Dresses
14	14	40	12	Dresses
16	16	42	14	Dresses
18	18	44	16	Dresses
4.5	4.5	38	6	Shoes
5	5	38	6.5	Shoes
5.5	5.5	39	7	Shoes
6	6	39	7.5	Shoes
6.5	6.5	40	8	Shoes
7	7	41	8.5	Shoes

WHEN DEPARTING

- Remember to contact the airport on the day prior to leaving to ensure the flight details are unchanged.
- It is advisable to arrive at the airport two hours before the flight is due to take off.
- If travelling by ferry you must check in no later than the time specified on the ticket.

LANGUAGE

The Republic has two official languages, English and Irish. Everyone speaks English, though you are likely to hear Irish in the Gaeltacht areas of the west and south (Kerry, Galway, Mayo, the Aran Islands, Donegal and Ring, and Co Waterford), where you may find road signs in Irish only. Irish is a Celtic language, probably introduced to Ireland by the Celts in the last few centuries BC. Below is a list of some words that you may come across whilst in Ireland, with a guide as to how to pronounce them.

hotel	óstán	(oh stawn)
bed and breakfast	loistín oíche	(lowshteen eeheh)
single room	seomra singil	(showmra shingle)
double room	seomra dúbailte	(showmra dhubillta)
one person	aon duine	(ayn dinnah)
one night	oíche amháin	(eeheh a waa-in)
chambermaid	cailín aimsire	(colleen eym-shir-eh)
room service	seirbhís seomraí	(sher-iv-eeesh showm-ree)

bank	an banc	(an bonk)
exchange office	oifig malairte	(if-ig moll-ir-teh)
post office	oifig an phoist	(if-ig on fwisht)
coin	bonn	(bown)
banknote	nóta bainc	(no-tah bank)
cheque	seic	(sheck)
travellers' cheque	seic taistil	(sheck tash-till)
credit card	cárta creidmheasa	(korta kred-vassa)

restaurant	bialann	(bee-a-lunn)
café	caife	(koff-ay)
pub/bar	tábhairne	(thaw-ir-neh)
breakfast	bricfeásta	(brick-faw-stah)
lunch	lón	(lone)
dinner	dinnéar	(dinn-air)
table	tábla	(thaw-blah)
waiter	freastalaí	(frass-tol-ee)

aeroplane	eitleán	(ett-ell-awn)
airport	aerfort	(air-furt)
train	traein	(train)
bus	bus	(bus)
station	stáisiún	(staw-shoon)
boat	bád	(bawd)
port	port	(purt)
ticket	ticéad	(tickaid)

yes	tá/sea	(thaw/shah)
no	níl/ní hea	(knee hah)
please	le do thoil	(le do hull)
thank you	go raibh maith aguth	(goh rev moh aguth)
welcome	fáilte	(fawl-che)
hello	dia dhuit	(dee-a-gwit)
goodbye	slán	(slawn)
goodnight	oíche mhaith	(eeheh woh)
excuse me	gabh mo leithscéal	(gov-mu-le-schale)
how much?	cé mhéid?	(kay vaid)
open/closed	oscailte/dúnta	(uskulta/doonta)

Acknowledgements
The Automobile Association wishes to thank the following libraries, photographers and associations for their assistance in the preparation of this book.

MARY EVANS PICTURE LIBRARY 10/11; **CHRIS HILL** 20/1, 56; **MRI BANKERS' GUIDE TO FOREIGN CURRENCY** 119; **NATIONAL MUSEUM OF IRELAND** 24; **NORTHERN IRELAND TOURIST BOARD** 85, 86, 87

The remaining pictures are from the Association's own library (**AA PHOTO LIBRARY**) with contributions from:
JAMIE BLANDFORD F/Cover: Dunmanus Bay, 5a, 12, 15a, 19, 23, 27a, 46, 54, 59; **LIAM BRADY** 12/13, 15b, 36, 42, 70, 83; **STEVE DAY** 1, 33, 37, 38, 63, 68, 71; **MICHAEL DIGGIN** B/Cover: statue, 5b, 53, 90, 122a/b/c; **DEREK FORSS** 51; **CHRIS HILL** F/Cover: farmer, 6, 60, 64, 82; **STEFAN HILL** B/Cover: door, 2, 9b, 16, 27b, 49, 52, 55, 73, 91a, 117a; **JILL JOHNSON** 8; **TOM KELLY** F/Cover: Four Courts, 7; **GEORGE MUNDAY** 26, 72, 76, 77, 79, 80, 81, 84, 88, 89; **MICHAEL SHORT** 18, 22, 30, 39, 40, 43, 45, 57a, 61, 91b, 117b; **SLIDE FILE** F/Cover: seal, 35, 41; **PETER ZOLLER** 17, 25, 44, 66, 67

Author's Acknowledgements
Penny Phenix would like to thank Terry Arsenault, her husband and business partner, for invaluable assistance with the walks and drives, for additional research and checking; also to acknowledge the assistance of Borde Fáilte, the Northern Ireland Tourist Board, various Tourist Offices throughout Ireland and Charleville Lodge in Dublin.

Contributors
Copy editor: Pat Pierce Page Layout: Design 23 Verifier: Jackie Rathband
Researcher (PracticalMatters): Colin Follett Indexer: Marie Lorimer